THE
CRANKY YANKEE

A collection of
columns, essays and true stories

VIRGINIA LEAPER

Cover artwork by Laura Leaper

1st WORLD
PUBLISHING

THE CRANKY YANKEE

Virginia Leaper

© Virginia Leaper 2008

Published by 1stWorld Publishing
1100 North 4th St. Fairfield, Iowa 52556
tel: 641-209-5000 • fax: 641-209-3001
web: www.1stworldpublishing.com

First Edition

LCCN: 2008925276
SoftCover ISBN: 978-1-4218-9862-9
HardCover ISBN: 978-1-4218-9861-2
eBook ISBN: 978-1-4218-9863-6

ABOUT THE AUTHOR

Virginia Leaper grew up in Rhode Island before moving to New York and pursuing a career in radio dramas and theater. Later she moved to California with her husband, actor Gerry Leaper, where she raised her family and occasionally appeared in stage productions and television commercials.

Virginia is widowed after a 58-year marriage and has two sons, three granddaughters and three great grandchildren. She lives in Wakefield, Rhode Island.

Dedicated to the memory of my parents,
Jack and Geneva Cheshire.

ACKNOWLEDGEMENTS

First, I want to thank Betty Cotter for her unfailingly valuable advice, inspiration, editorial assistance and support of my work, both as my employer and friend. To her, I owe my deep gratitude.

Also, for their important part in preparing the text for the computer disc, I would like to thank Chelsea Frederickson and Makayla Cunningham, always on time, always dependable.

Special thanks go to Chris Barrett for his diligence and efficient work in helping me navigate the difficult passage from manuscript to printed book. A task that called for many varied skills and reliability. His contribution was invaluable.

I would like to express my appreciation to all members of the South County Writers' Group, past and present, for their generous support. Special thanks to Richard Parker, Jeannie Serpa and Enid Flaherty, who were always on hand for consultation and valuable advice. Also included are Michael Grossman, Camilla Lee and Tracy Hart.

I owe a debt of gratitude also to Marie Younkin-Waldman and Myron Waldman, Linda Beaulieu, and Normand Leclair for willingness to share information based on their own publishing experiences.

And always in my corner, with loving interest, have been members of my family. Sons, Gerry and Jeff, their wives, Jan and Betsy, and granddaughters Jennifer, Janine and Laura.

Thanks, one and all.

CONTENTS

PART FOUR: AROUND THE TABLE

PART FIVE: A MOVEABLE FEAST

PART SIX: BETWEEN COURSES

PART SEVEN: SECOND HELPINGS

PART EIGHT: SALTY AND SPICY

PART NINE: REALLY TART

PART TEN: JUST DESSERTS

PREFACE

One of the nicest things about doing a column is hearing from readers, especially when they like what's been written. But even if they don't agree, it's good to know that at least some attention is being paid.

Two questions I often hear are, "How did you get started writing columns?" and "Where do you get ideas to write about?"

The answer to the first question goes back to Cranston High School where I started by writing short pieces in the school paper, *The Green Lantern*. It seems to me that I have always written. Eons later, when my husband, two young boys and I were living in California, I began a column called "Rhyme and Reason" for a weekly newspaper in the San Fernando Valley. At that time, I was also writing news pieces, interviews, and articles. After that paper was sold, I became what is known as a free-lancer, a euphemism for unemployed writer. This development had its upside, however, as it more or less forced me to send my work out to national markets and eventually get to appear in publications such as *Yankee Magazine, The Providence Journal, The Christian Science Monitor, The Ford Times,* and *The Los Angeles Times Sunday Magazine*. National Public Radio has also featured some of my work.

When the boys were grown and my husband, Gerry, took an early retirement, we came back here to Rhode Island, my home ground, and I began free-lancing pieces to all the local newspapers. After a while, I felt I really wanted to get back to writing a regular column again and when *The South County Independent*, with super managing editor Betty Cotter at the helm, began publishing in 1997, my column appeared in the first edition. I'm happy to say that "Rhyme and Reason" by Virginia Leaper has been showing up on the Op-Ed page regularly ever since.

As to the second question about where I get ideas to write about, I really can't answer that one. Sometimes from current events, sometimes from memory, often just one of those random wisps of thought that we all experience from time to time. Those are the ideas that you have to capture and write down notes, before they float away, never to be heard from again. Ideas are a mixture of everything from strongly-held opinions to nonsense, from sentiment to sarcasm. I do try to be honest, however, using the only thing any columnist has to offer, a view from one person's perspective, hopefully along with a bit of a story to go with it.

The pieces in this volume cover quite a lot of time since some are reminiscences and others are contemporary observations. I have tried to include columns which readers have been kind enough to respond to, and told me that they have sent to others.

To them and to all readers, I would like to say thanks for sharing your time with me.

Note: For purposes of relativity of events, the dates of publication of most of the essays and articles have been included along with the titles.

PART ONE

A TASTE OF RHODE ISLAND

THE RESTAURANT

October 9, 2003

Themes are very big these days. Just about everything from amusement parks to TV shows seem to have a gimmick. And in this spirit, I recently have been having a fantasy about a restaurant called The Cranky Yankee, a concept I could easily identify with.

Just inside the entrance of my imaginary eating establishment would be a small foyer, and on the customary easel usually presenting a list of the daily specials there would be a plain sign, reading:

THE CRANKY YANKEE:
WHERE ALL THE MEALS ARE SPECIAL

The waitresses would be mature professional servers. No bare mid-rifted college girls.

Not that there's anything wrong with that; they just wouldn't fit into the overall theme. On the menu would be all the New England dishes, which many of us remember from our early years. I would include as much as possible of the plain satisfying cooking that my grandmother served up every day when I was growing up, an only child, living with my parents and grandparents.

Annie Cranston, my mother's mother, was undisputed queen of the kitchen. My mother and I washed the dishes after a meal, but Annie did the cooking. Only a fool would have wanted it any other way. Legend had it that, at one time, she and Pa, my grandfather, ran a boarding house. Lucky indeed would those have been who lived there.

Despite her no-nonsense character, there was also a bit of the patrician in Annie, a quality often found in many otherwise down-to-earth Yankees. While no French chef, she had a lot in common with Julia Child. Coming from different backgrounds, they both could inspire awe with the air of confidence in which they occupied their space, the kitchen, where each reigned supreme. Upon occasion, Annie could also be somewhat cranky if interrupted while preparing a meal. I have a feeling that Julia, in spite of her unfailing good humor on-camera, could have shown a tad of irritation if annoyed, as well.

The main difference between Annie and Julia was that while the TV star was demonstrating how to turn out a masterpiece from the Cordon Bleu school of cooking, my grandmother would be making Yankee pot roast complete with jonnycakes, mashed potatoes, carrots, green beans, and sensational brown gravy. And when Julia prepared a fancy parfait dessert fit for a king, Annie would be rolling out the crust for a lemon meringue pie that would, as they used to say, melt in your mouth.

In addition to Annie's dishes mentioned above, the menu in The Cranky Yankee would include: Baked beans, cooked long and slow with salt pork, onion, and brown sugar. New England boiled dinner, corned beef cooked long enough to be tender but still sliceable, cabbage, carrots, potatoes, and beets. Served with horseradish and Annie's mustard pickle relish.

Finnan haddie … smoked haddock prepared with sliced onions, covered with milk and baked in the oven. Good with potato and a fresh green vegetable. Baked ham, with sweet potato, spinach, and applesauce.

Annie's Rhode Island (not Manhattan) quahog chowder made with salt pork cooked to crispy bits, onions, chopped fresh quahogs, including the juice, cubed potatoes, and tomato. Yes, tomato! This is not what they call New York style. It calls for a can of tomato but it is delicious and called red chowder. Authentically Yankee. No milk.

The menu would also include real chocolate pudding made with Baker's chocolate and cooked in a double boiler. Served with real whipped cream. Bread pudding with raisins. Fluffy yellow layer cake with homemade chocolate frosting. Indian pudding … deep dish apple pie … No matter what the entrée was, it was sure to be topped off with a fabulous treat. And when the holidays came along, with turkey at Thanksgiving and roast beef at Christmas, she went all out.

In those days, everyone came to the table with a big appetite and pitched in with gusto. If they had special needs, they didn't know about it and Annie was not temperamentally wired to cater to them anyhow.

When I was in my early teens, I once made the mistake of complaining that a piece of meat seemed a little tough. "It's tougher where there's none!" snapped Annie. 'Nuff said.

Pity the poor hostess-cook of today's holiday meal. Unless she has been forewarned, what a shock it must be to offer a traditional feast to a lineup of family and guests with all their dietary hang-ups. An imaginary group might include Uncle Clarence, a diabetic, Aunt Sally, multi-allergic, grown daughter Vicky, on a protein diet, her husband, Gary, high cholesterol, teenage daughter Deena, a vegetarian, her boyfriend, Mark (with the nose ring), a vegan. Add to this mix Vicky and Gary's two kids, who cannot disguise the fact that they would much rather be dining at McDonald's and you have a hostess's nightmare.

Things are different when you go to The Cranky Yankee.

Don't go there if you have special needs or are on a diet. This is a place to go if you would like to get some beef stew. When is the last time you had an old-fashioned bowl of beef stew served with a small loaf of home-baked crusty bread like your grandmother made?

Don't go there if you're looking for a big steak dinner with fries and a tomato salad. Sure, you may have a steak with a baked potato and some of Annie's fabulous cole slaw, and maybe creamed onions.

Don't go for fish, unless you want codfish cakes like you've never had, crusty and full of flavor, served with scalloped potatoes and fresh green beans cooked with a bit of salt pork, or maybe, on some nights, finnan-haddie baked in milk.

My dream restaurant featuring Annie's delectable comestibles may never materialize in real life, one reason being her reluctance to give out recipes. She was a master in the art of plain down-to-earth cooking but her directions, given out grudgingly, were of the pinch-of-this and small-handful-of- that, variety. Actually, she preferred not to be disturbed at her artistry, especially when asked to write something down. Also, she was to say the least, an original speller, given to adding unique endings to some words.

Thus, the only two recipes she wrote for me on faded lined paper, are preceded by a short note ending with, "Pa is getting cranky so I'll close and go fix his supper. Here is the chicking recipee you asked for and also one for the muffings."

Your grandma,
Anne G. Cranston

Needless to add, this note became a memento much cherished by this Cranky Yankee.

A LESSON BY THE SEASHORE

February 19, 1998

For a lowly clam
Or a bird that flies.
Tenacity
Can be unwise.

This story is a genuine "only in South County" tale. It came from an unimpeachable source, from my son Jeff and his wife, Betsy. And if that isn't enough, there were several other witnesses.

I guess you could call it a fish story. Shellfish, that is. Specifically quahog (pronounced "qwa-hog," not "coe-hog").

Now, quahogs, or *Venus mercenaria*, are not high on the scale of life forms. In fact, most people consider them to be just dumb clams, put here for the sole purpose of supplying the main ingredient of Yankee soul food, or "chowda." As it turns out, however, occasionally a super-clam comes along. And this is about one of them.

It was a bright sunny winter day, and along with a few other hardy souls, Jeff and Betsy were taking a pleasant stroll on Narragansett Beach. The tide was out, and since there had recently been a storm and a higher-than-usual tide, the sand was littered with stones. Here and there a marooned quahog lay patiently awaiting the next rush of water to take it back out to sea.

Up ahead of them, Jeff and Betsy observed a large sea gull pecking away at something on the beach. As they got closer, they saw that the bird was standing over a giant clam.

With the quahog's neck in its beak, the gull was energetically attempting to extract the clam's body from the shell.

Bemused, the strollers paused awhile to watch the tug-of-war. The gull pulled and pulled but the stubborn shellfish kept its trap shut and refused to surrender.

Enter the next player in this drama, a girl with a dog that was happily and noisily romping along the water's edge.

Up to now, the gull had been too preoccupied with the clam to pay much attention to the couple watching its struggles. The playful hound, however, was upsetting. Still grasping the quahog by its neck, the gull flapped its wings and took off a short distance, flying low over the rippling waves.

As the bird flew, the neck of the mollusk elongated and the weight of the big clam became too much for the gull. They landed on top of the shallow water.

Now, the tide of the battle changed. As the quahog hit the water, it realized it was on home turf. Like a retractable tape measure, it reeled in its neck. Pulling the gull's beak along with it, the clam closed its shell and sank beneath the gentle waves.

The bird was now the captive … its beak tightly held inside the bivalve, its head bobbing up and down in the water, it began to slowly drown. Its pure white wings, so strong and free, now spread helplessly atop the waves. Unbelievably, the powerful bird was about to become the victim of the lowly clam.

By now, Jeff, Betsy, and the dog walker had been joined by several other observers, watching the bird and the clam locked in a death struggle. The sight of the gull becoming weaker and weaker, tossing helplessly in the waves, became too stressful for the onlookers. "Can't you do something?" the women pleaded.

Jeff felt that action was expected of him. Removing his shoes and socks and rolling up his pant-legs, he waded into the icy water. The half-drowned gull was too far gone to offer much resistance and he managed to get it back to shore, its beak still stuck firmly inside the quahog.

Now, the rescuers were faced with one of those dicey dilemmas that occasionally confront us.

All efforts to open the clam's shell far enough to remove the gull's beak were unsuccessful. Finally, a rock was found and the clam was dispatched. Sadly, the underdog clam, who won the battle, lost the war, and the aggressor gull was set free. (If there's a lesson here, I guess it's about knowing when to let go.)

The quahog went to mollusk heaven, Jeff went home with mixed feelings and a bad cold, and the ungrateful gull, which had tried to bite him, flew off for home without a backward glance ... to say to his wife, "Honey, you'll never believe what happened to me today."

WHAT'S IN A NAME?

Spring 1999

Since ancestors of the Narragansetts and other Native American tribes have occupied this southern New England territory for at least the past 12,000 years, it's easy to understand why so many of our towns, waterways, streets and historic sites bear Indian names.

These are names that those of us who were born and raised in the area take for granted. Words taken from the native vocabulary may sound so familiar to our ears that we don't even stop to wonder what they mean. Visitors, however, often find them hard to pronounce and sometimes ask for a translation that may not be available.

Even the common word "quahog," our native mollusk, famous as the primary ingredient of our delicious chowder, is seldom known to mean "round clam."

Indian names can be found on street signs and maps just about everywhere you go in the Ocean State, especially in the eight towns, Narragansett, South Kingstown, Westerly, Charlestown, North Kingstown and Hopkinton, which make up the area known by locals as South County (actuality, Washington County, which also includes Richmond and Exeter).

Many times the place name may constitute a geographical description. Thus, Narragansett, the town, means "a point of land." Matunuck in South Kingstown translates to a "neck of land."

Charlestown, home ground of the Narragansett tribe, has many such places, including Watchaug, or "hill country," and Quonochontaug, (pronounced Kwana-Ka-Tog) meaning "long beach place."

Some places are named in honor of tribal leaders such as Ninigret, a war chief, and Canonicut, named for Chief Canonicus, the latter name to be found in the town of Hopkinton.

In North Kingstown, the important industrial facility and former base for the Seabees during World War II is named Quonset, which means "long place." A road in North Kingstown that also bears an Indian name is Annaquatucket, which means "at the end of the river."

Often, a place name may have more than one meaning. Thus, Escoheag in Exeter and West Greenwich is listed variously as "this is as far as the fish-spearing goes" or "a fork in the river where we fish."

Usquepaugh is the name of a tiny hamlet in Richmond where Kenyon's Grist Mill has for generations produced the white corn meal used in the preparation of Rhode Island johnnycakes. The mill was built on the Queens River and the current name was probably derived from the word Wowoskepog, which means "at the end of the pond." In the past, Usquepaugh was mistakenly thought to come from a Gaelic word meaning "good whisky."

Straddling Charlestown and Richmond is the village of Shannock, which means either "squirrel" or "where two streams meet." On the bank of the Pawcatuck River, there is a stone marker reading, "1636-1936 ... here the Narragansett Indians won a fierce battle against the Pequot Indians for possession of the fishing falls." This would have probably been over the bountiful supply of salmon in those waters.

Misquamicut in Westerly is another site once known as a "salmon place."

Occasionally, the same Indian name may be found in several locations. "Yawgoog," which can mean "red pond" or "as far as this place," for example, is the designation for a popular ski area, Yawgoo, in Exeter, as well as a Yawgoog, a pond in Hopkinton.

In Exeter may be found the Tomaquag Indian Memorial Museum. Tomaquag is the word for "they who cut" or "beavers."

Very often our Indian place names have to do with bodies of water. Thus, Saugatuck (Saugatucket River) in South Kingstown means "tidal river outlet" and Shickshinny (River) means "great spring."

Westerly's pond Winnapaug means "a great pond" and Wequapaug (Weekapaug) indicates "at the end of the pond."

In Hopkinton is the village of Ashaway, or "land between river branches."

Other descriptive features are also used, such as Narragansett's Pettaquamscutt, "at the round rock."

Many Indian-derived words have entered our everyday vocabulary. Massachusetts and Connecticut, for example, and words like squash, wampum, raccoon, moccasin, toboggan and succotash.

As a means of communication the Narragansett tongue is not extinct, Efforts to resurrect it and the language of other southern New England tribes is being made by people like Moon Dancer (Francis Joseph O'Brien Jr.) and Strong Woman (Julianne Jennings) of the Aquidneck Indian Council in Newport, who have put out "Understanding Algonquin Indian Words," a book that is available in libraries locally.

We are indebted to the founder of Rhode Island, Roger Williams, for the most important book on the Narragansett language, "A Key into the Language of America." Williams spent a great deal of time with the Indians, learning their customs, language and way of life. While on a return voyage to England, he wrote down what he had learned. Published in 1643, it was an invaluable historical document that is still useful today.

More information may be found in a book, "Indian Place Names of New England" by John C. Huden, published in 1962.

CLAMBAKE DAY

August 27, 1998

Late summer day.
Loved ones and friends,
A feast of memory
That never ends.

The early settlers who came to the shores of what was to become Rhode Island learned many things from the Native Americans living here. Practical things … about natural medicines, growing corn, hunting, fishing, and the rudiments of the much loved culinary art of the clambake. With the end of August in view and summer winding down, I can't help thinking about The Farm and clambake day.

I grew up in suburban Rhode Island but always loved the country. There were five of us at home: my parents, maternal grandparents, and me, the only child. When I was about six, Pa, my grandfather, began renting a vacant farmhouse from an elderly recluse in an area of South County called Nooseneck Hill. It was our weekend getaway place where we went in spring, summer, or fall, when weather permitted.

I could hardly wait to get to The Farm. It consisted of an old weather-beaten house without plumbing, a well with a rope and pail to draw water, an outhouse, a barn and lots of open meadows and rocks. We spent many a Saturday or Sunday there, never staying overnight, preferring the comfort of our own beds and other conveniences.

I loved the fields, long unfurrowed, where, in spring and summer, wildflowers burst forth. First, the big wood violets, buttercups, daisies, and later on, Queen Anne's lace, tiger lilies, black-eyed Susans, asters and goldenrod. There was also an old apple orchard, wild blueberries and grapes.

The house itself was sparsely furnished with a table, a few chairs, a wood stove and a few benches. In the parlor, there was an old pump organ that wheezed out sounds if you were able to manage the foot pedals.

Outside, under the trees, were long picnic tables and rough benches made of old boards. We always came loaded down with baskets of food prepared by my grandmother, a formidable cook.

In August, we would have the clambake when all the friends and relatives came to join in. Pa was the bake-master, the one in charge of the complex operation. Indians, who taught the art to the early settlers, would have called him Sachem of the Feast.

Under Pa's direction, the men dug a pit, lined it with rocks on top of which they built a wood fire. When the rocks were heated enough, in about two hours, the fire was raked out of the pit. Now, before the rocks cooled, they quickly spread a blanket of seaweed, which, along with the seafood, had been brought that morning from Narragansett Bay. Into the steam rising from the wet seaweed went the carefully layered ingredients of the feast, which were then covered by another layer of seaweed. A large canvas cover was finally placed over all and it was left to cook.

The women, meanwhile, were preparing the clam chowder made with the big Rhode Island clams called quahogs. We usually had a choice of the milk-based white, the clear, or the kind Gram made, the red chowder, which was my favorite.

Out under the apple trees, the women scurried back and forth from the house, setting out plates, cups and cutlery. The older children helped by keeping the young ones from underfoot and seeing that they didn't climb up to the barn roof or fall down the well.

In between their duties, the men pitched horseshoes. The air was rich with seaweed smoke, the sound of laughter, and the ringing of the iron "shoes" clanging together.

By the time we sat down to eat, everyone was famished and it took a lot of will power not to go for seconds on the chowder. Experience taught you to hold back or you'd never have room for what was to come. We all lined up at the bake site, where the men pulled back the canvas and the top layer of seaweed. Out came cheesecloth bags of "steamer" clams, small and succulent. We rushed back to the tables and ate these, liberally dipped in seasoned melted butter. Next came the portions of fish, white potatoes, yams, onion, sweet corn and lobster.

After this course, everyone sort of leaned back and rested before tackling the dessert. During this period, the lull in the eye of the hurricane of feasting, small pockets of conversation sprang up. Folks exchanging tidbits of information, bringing one another up to date on family happenings.

The ladies traditionally out-did themselves when it came to pies. There was sure to be blueberry, apple, rhubarb and peach. Each one was somebody's specialty. Then there were coffee for the adults and sarsaparilla or root beer for the kids.

When the dessert was finished, everybody lent a hand with the cleanup. After that, the men who were able went back to the horseshoe game, the boys threw a ball back and forth and my cousin and I went wading in the creek. A lot of others found a shady spot under the trees and fell asleep.

Late in the afternoon, when we were all standing around the packed-up cars saying goodbye, I remember looking back at the old worn-out farmhouse, the sagging barn and the covered well, the meadow with its late summer wildflowers surrounded by crumbling stone walls, and thinking that it must be just about the most beautiful place in the world.

Nothing in life, so far, has happened to change my mind.

CAN-CAN

September 24, 1998

*Harvest labor
deserved,
Summer sweetness
preserved.*

My next-door neighbor, Kathy, tells me she is canning tomatoes from her garden, an activity I mistakenly thought had gone out of style. It brought back a lot of memories.

Long ago, when harvest time came along and the little wild creatures were storing up food for the winter, I would surrender to a primitive urge to "put up" preserves and fill the larder with home-canned fruit and vegetables. Hypnotized by a Ball Mason jar pamphlet, showing a happy housewife in front of shelves of dazzling home-canned foods, I would plunge into a yearly session with jars, rubbers and kettles of boiling water. The house would be a mess, my family would go hungry and my disposition would deteriorate. At one time, I remember my son, aged 8, complaining about dinner being late.

"How can you expect me to stop and get your supper when I'm right in the middle of all this?" I shouted, indicating a kitchen strewn with canning equipment. "Don't you see I'm doing it so you'll have nice things to eat next winter?"

"But, Mom," protested my son, "we're hungry right now. How about one of these?" He picked up a jar of freshly canned peaches.

"Put that down!" I yelled. "And get out of the kitchen if you want to live to be 9."

Small wonder that shortly after this, our pride and joy took off one morning in the opposite direction from school, leaving behind a note stating that he was running away and "thanks for everything." (Luckily, he soon turned up at a friend's house and returned to his happy home and a hearty meal.)

I began my canning career early in my marriage in a little country town in Massachusetts where our house was surrounded by an apple orchard. In May, the trees were glorious with blossoms, inevitably followed by apples, thousands of them. I was pregnant, and the fruit and I ripened about the same time. I found myself barely able to reach over my stomach to the table, canning quarts of apples, applesauce, apple butter and jelly. I was not sorry when snow finally came and covered up the apples still on the ground,

Later on, we moved to California and bought a 1-acre "ranch" in the valley. One of the main features of the place was a small orchard, and the real estate agent assured us that the trees were just reaching maturity and would bear a good crop. Did they ever! About July 1 came the boysenberries. Millions of them. Luckily, friends with a freezer were able to take a lot of them off our hands. I only put up about three dozen jars of jam. Then came the peaches, nectarines, plums, and apricots. Not to mention the vegetables I had been reckless enough to plant. When we sold that place, I left all of the empty Mason jars in the basement with no intention of ever getting into that situation again.

Right! The next place, where we were to live for more than two decades, had a section of what had been a large planting of table grapes. Blue ones and red ones. Beauties. Made lovely jelly and jam, a whole lot of it.

Like my friend, Kathy, I've also canned a lot of tomatoes over the years as well. Rich in vitamins A and C and with half the calories of an apple of comparable size, the tomato did not become an acceptable edible in the United States until fairly recently. Although it was cultivated and eaten in Europe for centuries, here it was thought to be poisonous until, legend has it, a certain Robert Gibbon Johnson put fears to rest by eating a tomato on the steps of the courthouse in Salem, New Jersey, in the year 1820. No calamity befell Mr. Johnson, and the tomato's reputation was redeemed.

To many folks, even today, being able to look into a cupboard in winter and see colorful rows of produce, lovingly "put up" answers a primordial need as few less basic human experiences are able to do. So, if you have a garden burgeoning with the ripe red globes, more than your family can reasonably consume, it's a good idea to freeze some, can some, and look forward to that icy day in February when you'll proudly take from the shelves and open up a lovely jar of September joy.

MILLTOWNS AND DINERS

March 3, 2001

The disastrous fire that leveled most of the remaining 19th century wood and brick buildings that comprised the once-flourishing textile industry complex in Manville, Rhode Island is the most recent loss of historical landmarks in our state. Old mills and the villages that housed the workers of the past centuries were the heart of the industrial development in New England. It was here that immigrants from many other countries came to find employment and where many remained, raising children who eventually followed them into the mills. Now, the majority of these buildings lie abandoned, left to decay or fall victim to arson or vandalism. Luckily, a growing number are being converted to apartments, artists' studios, offices, or museums. A few have been saved by being given historic landmark status.

Reading about the mills brings back many memories of when I was a child and often rode along with my father on his business day-trips. My dad was a salesman working for a company that made small ceramic thread guides used in the textile industry. His territory was all over New England, but most of his customers were in Massachusetts, Connecticut, and here in Rhode Island with occasional trips to New Hampshire and Maine. My mother and I would sometimes accompany him and wait in the car while he called on the mill managers and purchasing people. I recall many hours sitting outside one or another of the huge buildings wondering idly what went on inside. Often strange smells and loud noises were forthcoming, but I had no clue about the long hours, six day work weeks and the low pay that made up the millworker's life … The overwhelming roar of the machinery or the hazards of inhaling cotton dust or being struck by a flying shuttle and other occupational hazards that the workers faced.

To my mother and me, those day-trips with Dad were happy excursions. We only went in good weather, of course, and during school vacation. We took along books to read and perhaps a snack or two, played word games and once in a while took a short walk while Dad was in the mill office. I remember seeing the rows of drab small dwellings and tenements that were built by the mill companies and developed into villages where the workers lived. Employees came from varied backgrounds. Many were French-Canadians but there were also Portuguese, Irish, and Polish, as well. Above the scene, like a gigantic potentate, sat the mill … a benevolent despot that provided them with employment but ruled their lives from cradle to grave, often for several generations.

We saw a lot of the New England countryside during those trips. Lovely woods, small towns and places like Willimantic, Connecticut, Manchester, New Hampshire, mill cities Lowell and Lawrence, in Massachusetts. In Rhode Island, among others, Dad stopped at Manville-Jenks, later destroyed by flood and fire in 1956.

There were factories that made woolen goods, cotton, silk, worsted. Often there would be a small room open to the public where they sold remnants and my mother, who made clothes for herself and for me, would sometimes buy a few yards of cloth. Crompton Mill, I recall, made the most beautiful velvet.

At lunchtime, Dad would stop at one of our favorite diners. This was always a treat. The shiny chrome and wood and linoleum interiors of the diners with wonderful aromas of food welcomed us. The dishes they served were substantial and delicious. Especially roast turkey or pot roast with mounds of mashed potato and lots of gravy.

I'll always remember their desserts: Apple, banana cream, peach pies or maybe chocolate pudding with real whipped cream. The atmosphere was unfailingly warm and convivial; the prices reasonable.

Sad to say, the roadside diner, one of the most nostalgic mainstays of those early days, faded from the New England scene when super-highways replaced the leisurely travel lanes, and the textile industry abandoned its historical position in this area and moved south where the owners were lured by a plentiful supply of low-cost labor.

These institutions and those who toiled in them served our developing country well. Wherever examples still exist, I believe they should be preserved as a valuable heritage for present and future generations to observe and appreciate.

WELCOME AND FAREWELL

July 3, 2003

Sometimes they come in Lincolns, sometimes they come in convertibles with the tops down. Often they arrive with families in formidable SUVs, sometimes (but not often) in beat-up jalopies. They have out-of-state license plates, most likely from Florida, New York, New Jersey, or Connecticut. They may also come on motorcycles, by train or bus.

The influx begins slowly around the middle to the end of May, depending on the weather, which in the present year hasn't been too enticing. But sometime, around the end of June, after few gorgeous, sunny, warm days, we natives look around and say knowingly to one another, "THEY'RE HERE!", and we don't know whether to laugh or cry.

It's one of those situations where there's a love/hate relationship. In this case, between us, the year-rounders, and them, the visitors. The merchants, summer-renting landlords and others who depend on them for income, of course are delighted to see the crowds on the beaches, the cars on the streets; the people waiting in long lines to get into restaurants, to be waited on in the post office and in the stores. To some of us, however, all of the above can be a pain in the you-know-what.

We may try to be generous. To be understanding. To go so far as to be happy that people can come here to our lovely little ocean paradise and find some solace and tranquility away from their frustrating and often frenetic lives. To see the kiddies frolic and play in the sand. But doggone it, don't they remember the golden rule? Pick up after themselves and their kids? Give the rest of us a break? And how about a little old-fashioned good manners? Less impatience and rudeness. A smile or two wouldn't kill them either.

They can be found browsing the antique shops and yard sales, dreaming of an appearance on the "Antiques Road Show" with a treasure that they bought for a song in Rhode Island. Conversely, the home folks are bringing out their white elephants with the fanciful notion that "those tourists will buy anything." A touch of larceny in the hearts of both parties.

In general, the visitors fall into several categories.

What I call the Metros, usually New Yorkers. They can be easily recognized by their upscale clothing, even beach wear. No doubt, they are really roughing it when they shop locally. They are easily recognized as they tend to wear large hats and small bikinis under loose cover garments. They are inclined to always be in a great hurry and avoid eye contact.

Next, there are the snowbirds, those with homes in Florida who often keep a beach house here (often going back generations). They figure they have it made, and they may be right. They appear to gloat when locals tell them about the kind of winter that we just had. To each his own, I say.

Then there are the day-trippers, the ones who live in nearby cities and just come down for the day or the weekend. This group can be the most destructive as they haven't invested in renting a house and don't feel any obligation to the locals since they won't be around long. They're the ones who will be paying for the trip by being caught in a traffic jam going home.

We locals tend to stay away from town as much as possible, avoiding impatient, impolite drivers and crowds in the shops. It is also disheartening to see such things as parking areas and public restrooms trashed.

Always eager to avoid crowds, I occasionally like to walk along the shore very late in the afternoon or early evening hours, when most of the people have gone. There may be just a guy searching the sand with his metal detector or a jogger or two. The beach and the eternal rhythm of the waves bring a sense of serenity. It is there for all to share.

As for the visitors, according to the Old Farmers Almanac, there will only be 18 sunny days this summer, so enjoy. We are glad to see you come and glad to see you go. Have a good time.

PART TWO

APPETIZERS

THE MYSTERY MAN

December 1997

What is real, and what is true?
I'm not sure I know, do you?
Some mysteries still give me pause,
Like who and what is Santa Claus?

Way back in the dark ages, when I was six and joyfully anticipating the approaching yuletide, a boy in my first-grade class began making insinuations about a fat jolly dude in a red suit that I found highly objectionable and downright slanderous. He was, in fact, questioning the actual existence of one whom I held in deep and reverent regard.

I had an urge to poke that little twirp in the eye with my pink pearl eraser, but since females had not yet achieved liberation, I just got sick to my stomach. I tried hard not to think about what he had said. However, as the saying goes, once the toothpaste is out of the tube, it's darned hard to get it back in again.

I was still upset, even after supper was over and Mama was sewing and Daddy had gone down to the basement, where he spent a lot of time fixing and building things.

Now, my aunt and uncle, our most prosperous family members, owned a rambling white Victorian farmhouse with a wide porch and a large living room with a fireplace. It was a tradition, each Christmas Eve, for all the children to assemble in the dining room and, at a signal from my aunt, the French doors to the living room would be opened and we would all rush in to be greeted by Saint Nick, who sat by the fireside with his bag of presents.

Waiting for those glass doors to open was very much like standing in the wings of a theater, listening for the cue to go on stage. The same heart-pounding breathless excitement. The theatrical similarity included special sound effects … hoof-beats, cries of "Whoa, there!" and the hearty "Ho, ho, ho's." By the time we got to go in, we were beside ourselves with anticipation.

Finally, we were allowed to enter and were immediately awestruck with the splendid tree, trimmed to perfection. And then there was Santa himself, be-whiskered and smiling, beckoning for us to come forward and receive a gift out of his sack.

In former years, when my time had come to approach, I had been too overcome with shyness to take a good look. But this time, I stared right into Santa's eyes and realized with a shock that Santa had the eyes of my mother's cousin Carl! It was true that Carl was a thin man, a war veteran who walked with a limp, but even I knew that under the red suit he could have pillows and that the beard could be a fake. The sick feeling I'd had at school came back and was still there a little bit even later on when we sang carols and had cookies and hot chocolate. I went to bed that night happy that it was Christmas Eve, but still troubled. I tried to stay awake for a while, listening for the sounds of a sleigh landing on the roof, but was too groggy and soon fell asleep,

When I woke up very early the next morning, it was still dark and the house very quiet.

Slipping silently out of bed, I tip-toed past the bedroom of my soundly sleeping parents, down the stairs and into the living room.

I had been guided by the still-glowing lights of the tree and, and there beneath it was the doll I had wanted! The one with the curly blonde hair (not straight and brown like mine). She wore a lovely pink dress of flowered material, which looked familiar somehow. And next to her was a wonderful dollhouse with windows and doors and a blue-painted roof. There was even a little table and two chairs and a bed. Santa was here! Santa had come through for me.

A little while later, after I had played with my toys, I sat on the couch, afghan wrapped around me, thinking about a lot of things. I thought about Santa up there at the North Pole with all those elves making toys in his workshop and Mrs. Claus helping him. And I thought about Daddy down in the basement and hammering and sawing and Mama sewing.

Daylight began to slip in through the living room drapes and, carrying my new doll, I went over to peek out the window. The ground was covered with new snow and it looked beautiful. Then I noticed something. Sled tracks. Wide ones, like those of a sleigh! They seemed to be coming from back of our house and across the street to the Hartmans' house. The Hartmans had five kids.

I stood there, staring, a sense of wonder sending shivers through me. Soon, the snow began to fall again ... big fat flakes that quickly covered up the tracks. I kept watching until they disappeared. Then I went sleepily back to bed.

That was a very long time ago, but I have never forgotten the wonder of that Christmas morning, when the world was new and anything was possible.

THE SNOWS OF YESTERYEAR

December 10, 1998

A young woman in California of whom I am very fond recently told me in a phone conversation that she has promised to take her two young children on a trip to the mountains soon. "My kids," she confesses, "have never seen snow!" I felt an instant pang of sympathy. No snow? An unimaginable situation to a New Englander.

In a child's world there are certain moments that remain lifelong memories of joy and expectation. That last of the school season and the first day of summer vacation. The excitement and wonder of Christmas Eve. The first time you found, after many tries, that you could ride a bicycle and, as it happened every year, seeing winter's first snowflakes.

For hours, days, weeks, even, you had searched the sky for impending snow. Then, one day, there it was! Rows of scalloped white clouds like mounds of mashed potatoes. A "mackerel sky," your grandmother called it. A sure sign that snow was on the way. Now you watched and looked out the window at every opportunity … at home or at school … tingling with anticipation but anxious. You wondered about the temperature. Was it cold enough? Could it turn out to be a false alarm? No, surely not. After all, it was almost Christmas time and you were hoping to get a sled. Outside, you sniffed the air. Yes, it smelled like snow, you watched and waited, and then, it happened. A feathery flake floated down … and another and pretty soon the air was full of them. You rushed in joyously shouting, "It's SNOWING!"

Of course, you would wonder why other people, adults especially, never seemed to be as happy about it as the kids were. But then, grown-ups were hard to figure out anyhow. Next, you would worry about what kind of snow it was going to be always hoping it was the kind that would stick and cover everything and get deep. You would fantasize about how it might get deep enough so you would be snowed in.

At an early age, I had been fascinated by the poem, Snowbound" by John Greenleaf Whittier, the 19th century poet, which tells of a blizzard that occurred when he was a child on his family farm. A verse includes the lines, "And, when the second morning shone / We looked upon a world unknown, / On nothing we could call our own. Around the glistening wonder bent / The blue walls of the firmament, / No cloud above, no earth below / A universe of sky and snow!" I thought how really great that would be.

Another thing the kids considered important was the quality of the snow that fell. There were several kinds. The wet sloppy kind not much good for anything; the light small powdery flakes that piled up but wouldn't stick together; and the ideal kind, a bit heavier, not too dry, and just right for forming snowballs or building a snowman. It was also the best kind for sledding.

I was lucky enough to live close to that beautiful spot sometimes called "The Jewel of Providence" Roger Williams Park, where there are many small hills for kids to slide down ... The park also had lovely ponds and lakes that, in those days, were often frozen over, making them perfect for skating. To my dismay, however, I found out, after a disastrous trip around a pond on my ankle bones, that I would never be a skater.

Most older people will assure you that winters were much colder and snow much more abundant in "their day." And they're right! In recent years, how many times have you seen lakes actually frozen over ... enough to make it safe to skate? And besides the now famous snowstorm of 1978, how many really deep, disruptive, honest-to-gosh blizzards? Nowadays, with 'round-the-clock' television and computer weather information availability, it doesn't take much of a snow prediction to send us all scurrying to the store for bread and milk, candles, batteries, and a fill-up at the gas station.

How different it was in poet Whittier's time, some century and a half ago, to be on a remote farm in the midst of a roaring snowstorm, the family drawing close around a fire as he describes it, "What matter how the night behaved? / What matter how the north-wind raved? / Blow high, blow low, not all its snow / Could quench our hearth-fire's ruddy glow."

Growing up, I heard many tales about tough winters. It was so cold that Narragansett Bay froze over shore to shore. My grandmother told me about when, as a young mother, she was riding in a sleigh with a runaway horse. Fearing for the life of her infant, she threw it into the snowbank. Luckily, they both survived.

I can remember times when snow covered our suburban street knee-deep. One time, especially. A boy and I had gone to a movie downtown during a snowstorm. When we came out of the theater, the snow was deep with drifts and blizzard conditions. We managed to catch the last trolley going to our neighborhood but the overhead wires had iced up and the trolley pole kept sliding off. Every hundred feet, the car would stop and the motorman and my date would have to get off and put the pole back on the track. We reached my stop well after midnight and found snow covering everything from porch to porch across the width of the street. Luckily, the boy was tall, and with him breaking the trail ahead of me, I finally got home.

As for those two little kids in California, I envy them their excitement at seeing snow for the first time, playing in it, enjoying it and hope they can always keep that feeling of wonder at one of nature's miracles.

THE TV CIRCUS

May 27, 1999

Indisposed. Housebound. Hitting the remote control. And what's on? Talk shows with lots of energy and ingratiating personalities, some genuinely interested in introducing guests with something of value to talk about or discuss. Good. Unfortunately, there are other programs seemingly designed to make fun of, and generally degrade, a sad string of kooks, whiners, pedophiles, cross-dressers and cheaters, all the grotesqueries of humanity. It reminds me of something from long ago. What is it? And then I remember.

As a child, I hated the circus.

Frightened by the animals and terrified of the clowns, I recall huddling miserably on the hard wooden bench, the unfamiliar smell of elephants and sawdust in my nostrils and a heavy sense of foreboding hanging over the scene.

Meanwhile, the other children in our family party, my cousins, were apparently having a happy time, laughing and chattering, bouncing excitedly up and down. I thought there must be something wrong with me. Animals were supposed to be exciting to watch, and clowns were supposed to be funny.

It was a thrilling and joyful time for most children and adults when Barnum and Bailey came to town. There was always an enthusiastic group of grown-up circus buffs on hand in the gray dawn hours when the train pulled into Union Station and unloaded the cars holding circus animals and gear. Later on, many would gather at the parade grounds and watch the swift, efficient setting-up of the tents and all the paraphernalia of the show. Next, around 10 a.m., came the parade. The calliope played a lively tune as plumed horses pulling beautifully decorated wagons bearing the caged animals rolled down the avenue. Other wagons held costumed performers and clowns smiling and waving to the crowd. Last to come was a line of gaily bedecked elephants. Then, in the afternoon, under the big top, there was the show.

Why did I always approach it with a sense of dread? Why did the thought of a red-wigged, wild-eyed clown coming at me holding a bunch of balloons make me sick to my stomach? I couldn't tell anyone. There were only inarticulate feelings.

I was appalled at the sight of people flying through the air, sure at any moment they would fall to their deaths. No wonder the pretty aerialist smiled and raised her arms in triumph when she successfully completed a maneuver and landed safely.

There were the wild animal acts with polar bears, lions, and tigers. The beautiful yellow-and-black-striped tigers up on their perches, snarling and pawing the air in frustration and hate for the whip-cracking trainer in jodhpurs putting them through their paces. Their wild hearts longing for the cool green jungles they would never see.

Inside the entrance to the main tents stood a huge cage with a sign, "Brutus the Great The World's Largest Gorilla." In the cage there was indeed an enormous ape. But beneath the glowering ridges of his brow, startlingly human eyes wearily looked out at the endless parade of people stopping to stare at him. Two species separated by time from ancient shared beginnings, complete mysteries to one another.

Lady bareback riders, tightrope walkers and clowns, always clowns, making lots of commotion with horns and loud explosions from backfiring vehicles.

And then, there was the sideshow. Housed in a separate tents was collection of human anomalies. In front, a barker gave his spiel: LADIEZ AND GENTULMEN! COME AND SEE THE MIND-BOGGLING SPECTACLE ... MONSTROSITIES YOU CANNOT EE-MAGINE." And behind him were big posters: The Dog-Faced Boy, The Tattooed Man, The Snake Woman, so-called "freaks of nature" garishly pictured.

That was many years ago.

Today, as I sample the lineup of some TV programs, sadly it would appear that not much has changed. As I once felt that the animals and the humans of my childhood circus days were mercilessly displayed, I see victims of human folly and frailty being grossly exploited on the talk and tabloid shows on a little screen in my living room, if I tune them in.

Luckily, there are many other choices available.

RUNNING BOARDS
AND RUMBLE SEATS

May 25, 2006

A trip with teenage friends in the 1930s.
(Virginia is in the rumble seat at left.)

"What's a running board?"

This question, once posed to me by a close female relative, set off a flood of memories. However, since talking about the "good old days" has been known to bore the blue jeans off the most rabid nostalgia buff, let alone a teenager, I managed to resist the impulse.

Instead, I went to my dictionary and read, "running board, a small ledge, step or footboard, beneath the doors of an automobile, to assist passengers entering or leaving the car."

This kept her quiet until a half-hour later when she suddenly asked,

"What's a rumble seat?" (It turned out she'd been reading a story with a 1930s setting.)

"Rumble seat," said my trusty dictionary, "a smaller open air seat behind the principal roofed seat in an automobile." But by this time, the damage had been done. These explanations were okay as far as they went, but they did little to convey the true meaning and essence of running boards and rumble seats. Only old-fashioned, first-hand reminiscence could do that.

I close my eyes and I'm six years old again back in my Cranston hometown. It's five o'clock in the afternoon and I'm sitting on the curb half a block from our house waiting impatiently for Dad to come home from work. Suddenly the car appears around the corner and he sees me and waves. I jump up excitedly and wait for him to pull over and let me climb on the running board. "Hold on tight, now," he says, and we roll gloriously down the street to the driveway and into the yard. Me, feeling like a winner.

Another time, it's a fabulous day in May. Golden sprays of forsythia, spring bulbs, and pink buds swelling on the sweetheart rose bushes. We decide to go on a picnic and the countryside is lovely. We come to a green meadow with mares and their new offspring and stop to watch the antics of the colts. "Let's have the picnic here," we plead, enthralled. Only then we discover that the grass is wet and the ground still muddy from the spring thaw. No place to sit or spread our picnic lunch.

"No matter," says Mama. She sits us down on the running board, passes out sandwiches, and we devour our lunch while the frisky colts provide a floor show.

Some years later, it's the day of the Big Game against our arch rival and our high school team has won. Drunk with conquest, we pour out of the stadium and pile into cars. Down Broad Street we roll triumphantly, each car loaded with kids inside and others, like myself, riding on the running boards, blowing horns and waving pennants.

As time went by, cars began to get more stream-lined and running boards were discontinued. Rumble seats, which had many purposes, bit the dust about the same time.

It's impossible, of course, to ignore the importance of romance in making rumble seats popular. They were great for making out (or necking, as it was then called). A rumble seat on a balmy summer night with a full moon had a kind of magic.

Besides their obvious appeal to romancers, fresh air fiends, for example, found them irresistible. New England weather could be tricky, however, and I remember riding ten miles in a rumble seat in the rain, trying desperately to keep an umbrella from turning inside out.

Anyone who has traveled with squabbling small fry in the back seat can appreciate the rumble seat as a great place to stash a troublemaker. Kids loved riding back there, anyhow. I know of one East Coast to California trip with two young battlers when I would have given a king's ransom for a rumble seat, but by that time, it was too late.

Photogenic appeal was something cars with running boards and rumble seats had aplenty. They've been featured in movies from the days when Keystone Cops hung from the running boards of flivvers to the "Bonnie and Clyde" and "Paper Moon" variety.

In snapshots, too. Glancing through any family album of the twenties and thirties and you'll find people posing with their cars. They made great props. Rumble seats with pretty girls in them; running boards with kids and dogs. In an old album, I had such a picture of Uncle Harry in front of his new auto, a big smile on his face, one foot planted proudly on the running board. I showed it to my granddaughter.

"Now do you know what a running board is?" I asked.

"Sure," she said. "It's a step."

A step back into the past, I thought. "Want to go get a burger?"

She put the picture down rather reluctantly and reached for her cell phone.

"Those times must have been really cool," she said.

LIGHT UP THE SKY
IN JUNE OR JULY

June 28, 2001

Well, June has "busted out" and is just about all over.

We've had a touch of every kind of New England summer weather, thunderstorms, muggy days and quite a few long, lovely ones when it was not-too-hot, just right. Lawns are green; flowers and weeds both growing like crazy and, unfortunately, so are the little critters that make life a trial for gardeners.

This year I decided to just plant a few token veggies among the flowers. These consisted mostly of one tomato and a single green pepper plant, a few shallots and basil plants, all of them gifts from a neighbor's overflow.

In addition, I put in a small section of lettuce and one of parsley with lavender and lamb's ears for contrasting color. Around this rectangle, I very loosely struck a 2-foot-high fence made from varied lengths of chicken wire formerly used for peas, thinking it would deter hungry varmints. It wasn't long before I discovered how wrong I could be.

I always enjoy looking out of my upstairs window in the early morning to get a glimpse of the garden in its various stages of development. Soon after making the plantings, I looked out one day just in time to see my old nemesis, the woodchuck (or one of his progeny), sitting saucily in front of the garden shed with a satisfied, just-dined expression.

Rushing down, I found out why. My lettuce plants had been gnawed to the nub and the parsley was reduced to bare stems. The rotten rodent had done the dastardly deed. He had somehow worked his way between the hastily erected sections of fencing to get into the bed. Luckily, with all the rain we've been having, lettuce and parsley sent up more leaves and made a fine recovery. I was not yet out of the woods, though.

On yet another fine spring morning, looking out the window revealed a rabbit daintily devouring all the blooms on the pansies, my favorite flowers. Again, I descended like an avenging angel (or devil) and chased the bunny, throwing a few random stones after him. My aim, unfortunately, is not good.

To cap the climax of this unfortunate seasonal drama, I also came down with a second bout of Lyme disease, having had it once before three years ago. It would appear that, although April had been called the cruelest month, June is not far behind. To date, however, the lettuce, parsley, pansies and myself are all doing well.

And now Independence Day is nearly here—the time for parades, picnics, barbeques and clambakes. The time for present-day public fireworks displays. Community affairs where families gather at town beaches or parks to "ooh" and "aah" as the magnificent pyrotechnics burst in the sky at a safe distance from the admiring crowds. There's no doubt that this method of celebrating represents progress and good sense, but there was a time when the Fourth of July was a day of excitement and some danger that kids anticipated for days before.

On the morning of the Fourth, we would awaken very early to sounds of firecrackers exploding all over the neighborhood. For quite a few days we had been buying, exchanging and trading fireworks that were for sale in every variety and hardware store.

My parents allowed me to buy as many as I could manage to fit in a big paper sack, and the selection called for enormous decision-making. There were, of course, cap pistols and caps to go with them. There were sparklers, pinwheels, fountains and sky rockets. I never chose the big firecrackers, which were favored by the boys, because the noise hurt my ears. I did, however, buy a few torpedoes, which exploded when you threw them on the sidewalk.

All day long, we would play with the noisy toys and, when darkness fell, it was time for Dad to take over and handle the big stuff. The pinwheels would be nailed to a telephone pole and lit to become a whirl of colored lights. The Roman candles would be lighted and held by the brave while sending forth their showers of sparks and fire, and finally sky rockets, their bases secured, would be set off to explode in a wondrous show of stars and colored lights against the nighttime sky.

It's true that there were always fires and often some serious casualties resulting from those long-ago celebrations. It's much better and safer today. But some of us will always remember the thrill of the old-fashioned Fourth of July, a day and night of excitement and joy right in our own front yards.

THE BIG SWINGER

July 30, 1998

I hope that I shall
Never see
A time when there are
Two of me.

Call me greedy, but in spite of having already had a goodly share of living, I sometimes despair because I won't be around to see and do enough, and especially to learn enough. There are times when I feel that my ignorance is profound and my experience limited. When I am jealous of future generations and all the knowledge that will be theirs.

Then there are other occasions, like right now, when I feel that I've learned more than I care to know, especially about doomsday asteroids possibly headed our way and news regarding the inevitability of human cloning. Subjects that I would gladly know nothing about. Subjects that make me long to return to a period of simple and happy-go-lucky innocence—like the time I saw the first "Tarzan" movie.

I was 13 and entering ninth grade. On a Saturday afternoon, a girl-friend and I went to what used to be Loew's State Theater (now known as the Providence Performing Arts Center), that great plush rococo moving-picture palace where every teenager's dreams of adventure and romance were projected on the gigantic screen, 10 times larger than life.

There was no TV, of course, and cinema attendance played a far greater role in people's lives than it does today. Movies provided escape from the work-a-day world, a taste of glamour both on the screen and in the ornate trappings of the theater itself, as well as the entertainment of the show.

Up to the time, I had been unaware of Edgar Rice Burroughs'

masterpiece of invention, "Tarzan of the Apes," and when I first got a glimpse of Johnny Weismuller swinging through the trees and yodeling, I'm afraid I went bananas for that ape-man. How I envied Jane! Like the teenage fans of today's "Titanic," watching the young lovers face the world from the ship's prow, I wanted to soar with Tarzan through the jungle. Just the two of us. (Frankly, I could have done without that annoying chimp.)

I was faintly aware that the whole concept of a human raised by primates was a tad unrealistic, of course, but was more than willing to put reason aside. I longed to sail over to Africa and find my own Lord Greystoke. When I rapturously described the movie to my father, he laughed. I was very cross with my father for a while.

Many years have passed since that time. And now we have movies that are fantasies, but also ones that could come true. And some, tragically, that have already happened. Gruesome and realistic war stories, holocaust stories, stories of slavery. And those that could happen, that show how a cosmic disaster could result in our becoming extinct like the dinosaurs. And, as far as I can see, there's not a whole lot that can be done about it. It's one of those things that makes ignorance seem like bliss.

Then there's that other bug-a-boo: human cloning. As repulsive an idea as can be imagined. Even as I write, I'm certain that there are books and movies being readied for public release on the subject and any day we will be flooded with them.

The most revolting aspect of this concept, to me, is the loss of individuality. The uniqueness in man and nature. When we are children, we are taught that no two snowflakes are alike. That each one of us is special and different from anyone else in the world. Indeed, the idea of oneness has become a basic foundation for most of civilized societies in recognizing the rights of every individual. Each person separate, one-of-a-kind.

So, I'm not planning on seeing any cloning movies or asteroid movies or gory war movies.

It's a jungle out there. Tarzan, where are you?

THE HAIR-DO

February 22, 2007

Recent news hot off the wire that singer Britney Spears is sporting a bald pate has, I imagine, caused some parents of young star-struck daughters with long luxurious locks to worry. Losing hair because of medical causes is one thing, but female head-shaving, as a publicity ploy, or as a teenage rebellion statement, is another.

I can't help remembering my first permanent wave. I was thirteen, starting junior high school (ninth grade then), starting to wear a bra. Given to turning beet red when called upon to recite. Longing to be a cowgirl in the old West with Gary Cooper shyly, yet passionately, in love with me. I sort of hung around the house a lot that summer before school began, reading movie magazines and getting on everybody's nerves. Looking over Photoplay and the other fan mags, and seeing the current crop of screen sirens who all seemed to be sporting gorgeous curly hairdos, I thought how wonderful it would be if I could somehow transform my straight brown locks into curls. Eventually, with some coaxing, my mother finally gave in and sent me to the hairdresser to get a permanent wave.

It cost $2, I remember, and took four hours during which I was attached by numerous wires to a machine designed by the Marquis de Sade, half suffocated by chemical fumes and the smell of burning hair. At the end, I came out looking like I'd stuck my finger in an empty light socket.

I cried for two whole days and wouldn't leave the house for a week. I washed it twice a day with copious amounts of hair coming out with each shampoo and Mother kept saying, "It looks *much* better," and Dad said, "Stick a bow in it and nobody will notice."

That's what he thought.

Aunt May took one look and burst into tears. "What happened?" she shrieked.

"Now, now, it's not that bad," Grandma said, crisply. "She can just wear a turban for while."

My friend, Teresa, tried to be reassuring. "You could look just like Helen Twelvetrees in 'Times Square Lady' if you were a blonde," she said. "Maybe we could bleach it."

I clutched my offending locks with alarm. "It already looks and feels and smells terrible," I moaned. "I'm never going back to school. And I'm never ever going to another beauty parlor as long as I live!"

The art of hairdressing has come a long way since those days. With any luck, you can now visit any modern salon and you won't come out looking like The Bride of Frankenstein. Of course, you won't get a perm for $2 either.

As a grown-up, it took me a long time to find a hairdresser I felt comfortable with. Moving from place to place over the years, I sampled many beauticians. Inevitably, upon meeting a new one, he or she would stand over me with a pair of scissors and ask the same question, "How would you like it cut?" This is probably my lowest point. Why not ask me to explain Einstein's theory of relativity or how to concoct a bouillabaisse? I haven't a clue. What I really wanted to hear was, "I've been studying your face and I know what's just right for you. Just relax, leave it to me and I'll make you gorgeous."

Good luck with that.

On occasion, I have been known to approach a perfect stranger in a restaurant or store and go right up and ask her where she got that great hairdo. Eventually, this bold move paid off. Using this method, I finally met Lorna, who, when we first began our cutting relationship, was a young newly married, helping her husband build their home. Today, she has a daughter in college and a son finishing high school. Nobody can call me fickle.

Then there's the subject of wearing a wig, which may be the way Britney could go if she gets an unhappy reaction to her new look from her many fans and followers.

The last time I owned a wig was some years ago in Hollywood, when I worked in a commercial starring the Tonight Show's Ed "Heeeere's Johnny" McMahon. My part called for a brief appearance as Ed's partner in a bridge game.

Except for Ed, this was not a big budget commercial. In accordance with requirements of television, however, we had the usual union specialists, including a make-up man. When this character was done with my face, I withdrew my wig from its case.

"I wonder," I said, "if you could give me little help putting this on. Maybe put in a couple of pins or…"

I never finished. The man threw down his powder- puff and leapt back as though I had made an indecent proposal. Straightening up to his full 5 feet 6 inches, he glared at me.

"I don't do hair!" he said, icily.

It just so happens neither do I.

HELPING KIDS

May 17, 2001

KIDS! I don't know what's wrong with these kids today!
KIDS1 Who can understand anything they say?
KIDS! They are disobedient, disrespectful oafs! Noisy, crazy
sloppy lazy loafers!

The lyrics of the above song, written by Lee Adams and Charles Strouse for the 1950s Broadway show, "Bye Bye Birdie," echo sentiments from the past when teenagers were irritating parents with rock' n' roll music and baggy clothes instead of spreading terror with guns and insulting teachers with specific songs about them on the internet.

Some of today's parents and grandparents who were those kids of the '50s may consider their era as the good old days, and echo another part of the song's lyrics: "Why can't they be like we were, perfect in every way? What's the matter with kids today?"

Of course we, all of us from any era, know that as kids we were far from being "perfect in every way." And like today's parents, our elders often felt we were going to hell in a handbasket (whatever that is); only now, some of our kids really are. The hell of addiction, prison terms and mixed-up lives, all provided by adult greed, selfishness and bad judgment. Modern life, with its de-emphasis on what are now considered quaint and antiquated values such as moral and religious codes and putting family solidarity ahead of material acquisitions, laid the groundwork for a multitude of young people to become alienated and lose their way in the frightening and lonely teenage years.

Between the ages of roughly 11 and 17, a youngster enters a period of momentous physical and psychological growth. Hormones flood into the systems of both boys and girls. The body undergoes changes, some welcome and some distressing. In the mind, the emerging adult struggles with the child still within. Strong emotions sometimes become overwhelming. Often, it seems, beyond understandable provocation.

I remember when I was around 15 and a boy in school named Eddie, a boy I scarcely knew, had an auto accident and had to have his foot amputated. I felt the trauma of this incident with an intensity that caused me sleepless nights and as much sorrow as if it had happened to a close family member. Eddie finally came back to school, fitted with a prosthetic and apparently in good spirits. It took a while, however, for me to recover from the shock of knowing such a thing had happened. Just imagine the emotional damage that the tragedies at Columbine and other schools must have imposed on the survivors.

Embarrassment and humiliation are also emotions young teens experience before their feelings develop that protective layer of insulation that makes adulthood bearable. Beginning junior high school, I found being elected chairman of my homeroom and conducting a weekly meeting in front of the class so overwhelming that I once fled from the room and had to be rescued from the hall by the teacher. Mercifully, the memory of having to return to the class has been erased by time.

Such trivial emotional upheavals from long ago bear little resemblance to what seems to be happening to youth today. Dysfunctional families, the easy availability of guns and drugs, the elevation of irresponsible role models from media and the constant bombardment of violent movies, TV games, and television programs surely contribute greatly to the tragedies.

I believe that we cannot overlook the responsibility we all share in providing a safe and solid basis … a background of support, understanding and love in the first formative years of a child's life. This is suit of armor that can be invaluable later on when he or she hits the roller-coaster of teenage emotions, the fantasy world in which, to a few lost kids, the distinction between life and death loses significance, where the temptation to destroy a tormentor becomes too great and there is no perception of consequence.

We all are aware that for every seriously mixed-up child there are hundreds more who are able to cope with their problems. Let's keep the lines of communication open to all of the youngsters who may need a little help. Talking to your kids is good; listening and occasionally reading between the lines may be even better.

Most important, making sure they understand the difference between right and wrong and have a strong sense of support for others, especially teachers, would be the best idea of all.

PART THREE

SALAD DAYS

A BITE OF THE BIG APPLE

Having a recent high school graduate in the family brings back many memories, especially of that in-between period which follows the celebrations and the parting of old comrades and the start of the responsibilities of the new life.

Young people today may not be aware that going to college was not always as much an attainable opportunity as is common today. The first year after I graduated from high school was spent sporadically working at low-paying jobs and taking a weekly drama lesson with a fine teacher from Pembroke College. Miraculously, through the sponsor-ship of my teacher, and the support of my parents, I was able to spend the next two summers as an apprentice at The Berkshire Playhouse in Stockbridge, Massachusetts, at that time one of the leading summer theaters in the East.

It was at a time when many of the now-legendary figures of the literary and theatrical world were at their peak. Sinclair Lewis, Alexander Woolcott, Tallulah Bankhead, Ruth Gordon, and Ethel Barrymore were some of the luminaries who came to the beautiful little town in the Berkshires. It was an entire dramatic education in itself to be able to sit every evening for a week in that darkened theater and watch Ruth Gordon spin her magic into her characterization in "The Church Mouse."

On Saturday afternoons we students went up to Jacob's Pillow for the weekly dance exhibition put on by the famous Ted Shawn and his troupe. We sat cross-legged on pillows on the floor and watched the powerful male dancers in routines that were later seen by audiences all over the world. On weekdays, one of Shawn's troupe came to the theater and put us through a strenuous workout every morning.

Blanche Yurka came up to the barn near the Playhouse, which served as our classroom, and graciously entertained us with impersonations and examples of pantomime. A star of the Yiddish Theater gave us lessons in the art of make-up. We rubbed elbows with the great and the near great of that fabulous world and hourly breathed that special air. It was heady wine for a bunch of stage-struck kids.

A great deal of our conversation in those days was devoted to making plans for going to New York in the fall. Some of us, the lucky ones, did.

Although many may insist, with some truth, that The Theater exists wherever there is a performer and an audience, it is somehow impossible to separate Theater from New York or vice versa. It is the Mecca toward which all those who were ever bitten by the bug bow in reverence.

To young people who are laboring in the kindergarten of the theater and seriously learning their art, I would say, you haven't lived until you have walked the rounds off Times Square and inhaled the brisk fall air and felt the fever of hopes rising all around you.

Go East, young man or young woman, when you are ready, and don't worry too much about whether you'll ever become a shining star.

It is something just to have been a part of it.

TIMING

February 24, 2006

When you reach a certain point in life, you tend to indulge in quite a lot of reflection. Sometimes you reflect on serious stuff, like how much your life has been determined by timing and chance, how differently things might have turned out if this or that had or hadn't taken place. Then, of course, there's the role that time itself plays in our everyday lives. Deadlines to meet, appointments to keep. We can't escape it, even in trivia. For example, have you noticed lately how long the commercial breaks in TV programs are?

It used to be that when a commercial came on, you just about had time to run to the kitchen and grab a bag of chips, or possibly use the bathroom, if you were quick. Today, the breaks are long enough to give you time to place a phone call, make a sandwich, and also visit the bathroom, if so inclined. By the time you come back, you may have lost the thread of the program and are ready to switch channels anyway.

When we think about time, there are plenty of axioms to peruse, from Shakespeare's "I wasted time, and now time doth waste me" and the ever popular "Time and tide wait for no man," to Thomas Paine's "These are the times that try men's souls," my favorite and very appropriate for the times we're living in.

How we use our time is what's important. I recently came across an article that described a good way to allocate time and effort. It was to employ what's known as the Pareto Principle, or the "80/20 Rule," which is based on the idea that 20 percent of the things we have to do really matter and the other 80 percent are trivial. The rationale, which the article states is used successfully in businesses around the world, is that concentrating on the important 20 percent and spending less time or no time on the rest, is the way to go.

Along the same line, I have for a long time been using my own scale to judge how concerned I can allow myself to get about the multitude of problems ... personal, national and worldwide, that are out there.

Thinking about a particular situation, I ask myself:

1. Is it important?
2. What, if anything, can I do about it? And:
3. How much can I afford to let myself worry about it?

Unfortunately, the answers very often are Yes, Not much, and Very Little.

Going back to the original subject of how destiny sometimes depends on time and chance, I'm reminded of a snowy day many years ago when a friend and I, young aspiring actors, trudged the streets of Broadway in New York hoping to see a casting sign outside a stage door. Finding none, and after meeting other hopefuls in Walgreen's and talking theater talk over one-shot cups of coffee for as long as we could string them out, my friend and I left, bought a newspaper and went over to another hangout, the lobby of the Hotel Astor, where, ignoring the desk clerk, we sat down and went through the ads. One caught my eye, a casting call for a theater group in Greenwich Village having auditions that very night. We mulled over the prospect. It was going to be a bad night. Deep snow and still falling. I wasn't crazy about going and neither was my friend, but we finally decided we should. You probably guessed it. We went. We got jobs. But, best of all, I met him. Another actor. The One with whom I was destined to spend my life. Time and chance. They worked for me.

RADIO DAZE

November 16, 2000

Recently, I re-discovered the joy of radio. I must admit to having neglected the small box for years, mostly because I cannot abide talk shows with call-ins, and also when I take a break from work, it is so tempting to respond to the siren song of television.

One evening, however, after a frustrating tour by TV remote through a serious of vacuous program selections being offered on the tube, I turned on my radio and was instantly delighted and soothed by an evening of classical music, which I hadn't realized was available in the evening. Since then, I have become more picky about what I watch on television knowing there is a very pleasant alternative to choose. One that offers a bonus. You can enjoy listening to music while reading a book.

Back in what young people would consider the dark ages, before the introduction of television and the electronic age, radio played a big part in daily life. Besides regular news and sports reports, listeners were treated to a rich and varied smorgasbord of programs, dramas, variety shows, comedy and entertainers like Amos and Andy, Kate Smith, Fred Allen, Edgar Bergen, Jack Benny, Eddie Cantor, and music of all kinds.

By the mid-1920s, Dr. Walter Damrosch, leader of the New York Symphony Orchestra, had already conducted the first full symphony concert on the air and was presenting programs with selections from Grand Opera. He was also becoming famous for his Saturday morning children's series, "The Music Appreciation Hour," which he opened with the familiar introduction, "Good morning, my dear young people" and to which young and old alike tuned in.

Before long, in addition to classical music, there would be the popular music of the day. Orchestras like the Cliquot Club Eskimos and the A&P Gypsies, crooners like Rudy Vallee, and dance bands like Paul Whiteman's Orchestra, jazz and show tunes. The thirties and forties brought in the sound of the big bands led by Glenn Miller, the Dorsey brothers, Harry James, and Glen Gray and others … as well as singers like Bing Crosby, Sinatra, and Ella Fitzgerald, incomparable all.

One of the great things about the time when radio reigned supreme was the delicious challenge to the listener's imagination. This was the tine when a scary drama on a program called "Lights Out," crafted by some very clever writers, could frighten the daylights out of an audience sitting safely in their darkened living rooms. What you could imagine was a lot more inventive than what you might see on a television or movie screen. Audience participation also added impact to comedies. In a show called "Fibber McGee and Molly," for example, listeners could readily envision the moment in every episode when the man of the house, Fibber, would open the door to his closet and a loud and raucous clanging and banging followed. Every person who heard the noise could picture the boxes, the mops, the old hockey stick, the tennis racket, the toys, the odd pots and pans…all the clutter that is present behind some door in everybody's house came spilling out. It was a hilarious moment and Fibber McGee's closet became part of folklore.

Just as TV does today, radio had its share of soap opera fans, and they were well-supplied with a menu of dramas. At one time, there were daily 15-minute episodes of as many as 35 different serials being broadcast from New York. Advertisers' target audiences consisted mostly of housewives at a time when relatively few women worked outside the home (there was plenty of work to do right there).

My husband-to-be and I spent some hectic time working in New York with a handful of other actors, doing a show for a home-diathermy sponsor (I never did find out what diathermy was). The 15-minute daily show was written the night before the broadcast and we were allowed time for one reading and run-through of the script before we went on the air. Ours was not a serial with an on-going story line, but consisted of a separate short story every day, which meant that the actors never knew what character they were playing until a half-hour before the broadcast. It kept you on your toes. This took place in a mostly bare studio room with the writer-director and the soundman with his table of noisemakers available for slamming doors, tooting horns, barking dogs and such, by his side.

Naturally, there were plenty of glitches but it gave us lots of experience and great memories.

RELATIVELY SPEAKING

March 25, 1999

As we all know, the English language has undergone some drastic changes in the last few decades. Words now have different meanings than heretofore. Take the word "relationship." It used to mean a connection to a family member, your parents, grandparents, siblings, or a spouse, for example. Or a relationship could be a business arrangement or an impersonal or purely social tie. But today's use of the word with a non family member of the opposite, or same gender, usually implies a sexual involvement. I must admit it has a nice refined ring to it. "Having a relationship." A great improvement over the old crudities that we all remember.

There are also a number of subtle distinctions. The person one has a "relationship" with may be known as his or her "significant other." A designation that goes beyond the elementary boyfriend or girlfriend status and occupies a position close, but not equal to, fiancé or fiancée. Here, clarification is called for. Some of us may still be unsophisticated enough to imagine the latter terms mean that wedding bells are imminent. Not necessarily. We are talking here about words, not action. The "engagement" may last longer than some marriages, and vows may never be exchanged.

A case of arrested development? Balking at the hurdle? What's the big deal? There's still the "relationship" (until it wears itself out). Nobody's committed. Nobody's hurt. Are they?

Maybe not. Not if they are people in their middle years or older. People who are looking for companionship and affection. Those with valid reasons for not wanting or needing a deeper involvement, like children. But for young people, it can be a trap.

The dating game, which leads to the "relationship" game. The investing in a no-hope situation. The moving in together, setting up a pseudo-domestic tableau. The eventual dumping or being dumped. Repeating this scenario desensitizes. Wounds. A twisted, tortured distortion of the natural order of things once practiced in cultures throughout the world. Which begins with the attraction, male and female, then the courting phase, its excitement enhanced by anticipation, not consummation.

The plighting of troths (to use an ancient phrase) moves the pair onto another plateau. Ready to take on the pleasures and pains and responsibilities of the journey of life. Not always success, of course. Some fall, some fail, some fulfill the promise and reap the rewards. Homes, children, all the great and small moments of joy for which the heart yearns.

It's no news that all of life is a gamble. But a gamble with some rules seems better than a shambles without any. Rather like repeatedly preparing for a play, in which cast members may be replaced, scenes written, rehearsals continued, but the curtain never goes up.

The fulfillment we all seek, illusionary, perhaps…but necessary as breathing, comes with some pain and much struggle. Yet feather-light and strong as steel, when two can say, "I do" and mean, "I'm here for the long haul. You can count on me."

THE VOWS ARE CONTRACT ENOUGH

February 4, 1999

To those of us who write with any degree of success (which means we get published with some degree of regularity) the temptation to pontificate can be strong. Especially considering the enviable success of books that tell readers how to live their lives. A glance through the best-seller list shows tomes on how to be more attractive, lose weight, get along with other people, get married, get divorced or raise kids, to name just a few. Then there are the ever popular feel-good treatises, the "Don't Sweat" (the small stuff etc.) and "Chicken Soup" (for just about everybody's soul) series. It appears that if you can be a convincing know-it-all, the world will beat a path to the bookstore to get your advice.

Of course, it helps if you have a string of impressive credentials, i.e., Ph.D.s, M.D.s or any other combination of academic letters after your name. Lacking any of those, I have decided to make up my own accreditation. I will henceforth be known as V. Leaper B.T.D.T (Been There Done That), which somehow makes me feel confident to explore a broad range of subjects.

Take marriage, for example. It seems that traditional marriage is getting a bum rap these days. There are those who contend it is outmoded, its demands are unrealistic and should be altered to fit the times. One pundit has put forth the idea of drawing up individual contracts, custom designed by each couple, outlining in detail just what responsibilities each person would and would not agree to. In a fully legal document.

This idea conjures up a very complex union. After changing the main points of the ceremony, which cover marital fidelity, devotion in times of trouble and ill health, and duration of commitment, the new kind of agreement would have to determine who would assume duties such as paying the bills and taxes, cooking, shopping, cleaning; who would change the babies' diapers and how often; take care of the car(s), walk the dog, empty the cat litter; the whole spectrum of domestic minutia ad nauseam. Hearing of this plan, one lawyer said it would take 50 pages to draw up such a document and perhaps 20 years to negotiate. A lot longer than many marriages last.

What's so great about marriage, anyhow? Marriage is admittedly a setup. It sets you up to commit yourself to taking a place of responsibility in the world and in society. The marriage ceremony, even the most pared-down conventional version, has a beautiful simplicity.

"Do you, John, take this woman, Mary, to be your lawfully wedded wife?"

"Do you, Mary, take this man, John, to be your lawfully wedded husband?"

"To love and comfort … to honor and keep in sickness and in health … for richer or poorer … forsaking all others … faithful to each other … until death do you part?"

"I do."

"I do."

Now there is a unit where once there were two unfocused, uncertain human beings. Now there is a foundation upon which to build a family and a future.

The idea of marriage has a lot in common with a democracy. As imperfect as it may be, it's the best we have come up with so far. Both concepts have evolved through time with the sole purpose of preserving our species.

Marriage was an attempt to ensure the nurturing of the human infant, that most helpless and vulnerable of creatures. I am not so naïve as to believe that getting married is a guarantee of stability, but it is a promising start for a man and a woman and an invaluable background for a child.

Today, many marriages fail. Some believe the "me" factor, the concentration on individual goals, selfishness if you will, is responsible. Not enough love and caring for another person's happiness and welfare.

I'm glad that I remember a young couple who stood together one

June day in City Hall in Philadelphia. It was Constitution Day, a holiday in that city, and a judge presiding over traffic court was the only one available to perform a quick marriage ceremony between cases. Standing behind the couple were several burly, smiling policemen and a few traffic violators. No family, no friends … just the two of them as they were pronounced man and wife. A court photographer snapped a picture and strangers offered congratulations. For a honeymoon, they went to a movie.

They were broke; they were in love; they were happy and unafraid of the future. The world was their oyster.

That marriage, replete with joy, sadness, devotion, fighting, making up, understanding, irritation, support, mutual admiration and lots of love, lasted for life.

I'm still asking myself, how lucky can a person get?

Virginia Cheshire and Gerard Leaper are married on June 21, 1938 at Philadelphia City Hall. The wedding portrait was taken by a newspaper reporter who happened to be in court that day and wrote a story about the couple's unconventional wedding.

CATALOGS OF HOPE

January 8, 1998

To overcome
That winter gloom,
Picture a garden
Filled with bloom.

W hether we like it or not, the mantle of January is upon us. We have already passed the winter solstice, and the year's shortest day has come and gone. Those of us who can't stand what may be on the way have already left for sunnier climes and the tougher ones are prepared to grin and bear it.

To some kids, skiers and nature lovers who glory in a snowy landscape, this can be a prime time of year. Others suffer from all sorts of psychological and physical downers during the darkest parts of the season, January and February, and go into a kind of a mental hibernation until spring. There are bright spots, however, and one of the brightest is happening right now.

The garden catalogs are beginning to arrive!

What is more uplifting on a snowy, slushy, dark day than a gloriously illustrated brochure full of colorful blooms, impossibly perfect vegetables and flowers? Even when you know that your new gardening efforts will probably never even come close to this vision, you can plan and hope. To anyone who gets a thrill out of seeing their seedlings sprout or the green tips of those spring bulbs pushing up through the soil, the catalogs are a joy.

To me, they were once much more than that. My husband and I were young, newly married, and living in a rooming house. It was midwinter, times were tough and our high hopes had lost the first round in battle with stark reality. He had a job far removed from his chosen field and my holiday season job was terminated. I was spending more and more time sitting in our one room, complete with stove and refrigerator, bathroom down the hall. It was a very snowy year, and on Valentine's Day there were 3-foot drifts outside our city windows. During this stark season, both my beloved grandparents passed away. Depression began to settle in as insidiously as a winter chill.

At some point, while vainly searching the want ads, I came upon a newspaper ad for seed catalogs and, for no particular reason, sent in a postcard. A couple of weeks later, lo and behold, they came! Gorgeous pictures of brightly colored flowers in gardens bordered by green lawns. Starving for something, anything to lift my spirits, I devoured the pictures and the descriptions. I studied the plants and memorized the names. One flower especially appealed to me, California poppies (*Eschscholtzia californica*). These silky, orange-petal beauties, which I had never seen before, seemed to embody springtime. I vowed that I would someday grow them in a garden. I had no way of knowing that in a few years I would live in California and would see windswept fields of those poppies growing wild in the foothills of the Sierra Mountains.

My involvement with the catalogs took my mind off our problems and I began to draw diagrams of gardens with names of flowers I would plant. I now knew the names, colors, the height and the growing requirements of many flowers. I could almost smell the fragrance of the roses and the spicy odor of the carnations.

With pen and paper in my hand, I also began to revive an interest I had had at school. I began to write … My early efforts often met with rejection. But it was a start.

As the weather improved, so did my husband's job prospects. We managed to buy a used car and found a cottage to rent out in the country. As soon as the ground could be dug I planted my garden with seeds, including California poppies, I had ordered from a catalog.. The time I had spent in that one room, writing, also began to pay off. I sold my first story and a song of mine was included in a radio broadcast from New York, sung by a well-known vocal group.

Since those days, I have had gardens in many places. Patio gardens in cities like Boston and Brooklyn in the east, in Hollywood and Santa Barbara in the west. Bigger ones in the San Fernando Valley and currently, my mid-size one here in South County.

Now, looking through this year's crop of catalogs with their seductively pictured posies and produce, I know that no garden of mine will ever achieve that lushness. But like gardeners everywhere, sitting indoors snug and warm, I can dream.

A HOLIDAY'S STRANGE HISTORY

February 14, 2002

My funny valentine
Sweet comic valentine
You make me smile with my heart.

—*Lorenz Hart*

Valentine's Day is all about love, about hearts and flowers, boxes of candy, pretty jewelry and presents for your beloved. Right?

How about wolves (the four-footed kind)? Roving packs of voracious, predatory creatures that once roamed the hills outside Rome, waiting for a chance to pounce on the flocks of sheep grazing there and snack on a shepherd or two. It's a legend but probably rooted in fact. The beginnings of St. Valentine's Day had more to do with Red Riding Hood than Cupid.

Around the third century, a pagan god, Lupercus, was believed to protect the sheep and shepherds from wolves. So, in February, a feast called Lupercalia was celebrated to honor him. Later on, Christian clergy wanted their converts to abandon the heathen gods so they changed Lupercalia to St. Valentine's Day.

There were actually several Valentines who qualified for sainthood. The most prominent was a bishop of Rome who stood steadfast against tyranny during the reign of the infamous Emperor Claudius. Valentine was put in jail, where he is said to have cured the jailer's daughter of blindness. When the miracle was made known, he was beheaded.

Another version has Valentine falling in love with the jailer's daughter and sending her letters signed, "From your Valentine." In Italy and Germany, people pray to another St. Valentine to cure them of their epilepsy.

An early Christian ritual involved a priest placing names of different saints in a box. Young people drew these names out, and during the following year each youth was supposed to emulate the saint whose name was drawn.

Eventually, a custom developed of substituting the names of maidens for those of saints, and when a youth drew a girl's name, he wore it on his sleeve and became her protector for a year (that might be where the phrase wearing your heart on your sleeve came from). After a while, they began to decorate the paper on which the names were written and wrote messages as well.

Seventeenth-century lovers presented their sweethearts with flowers, lacey valentines, heart-shaped candies and even more substantial gifts like jewels. In the Victorian era, the valentine rage became really elaborate, with gold and silver lovers' knots and golden hearts. The custom waned somewhat overseas until American soldiers revived it when they were stationed in England during World War II.

In this country, the first valentines to catch the public fancy were created by Esther Howland, a student at Mount Holyoke College more than 150 years ago. Esther's father imported valentines from England to sell in his shop. Esther decided to whip up her own version using imported lace and fine materials. These became known as Worcester valentines and were a huge success. They are now sought-after collector's items.

Around the time of the Civil War, Valentine's Day ranked second in importance only to Christmas. Beautiful valentines, hand-painted and trimmed with fine lacework, were produced during that period.

Our cards today may not be that fancy but are still fun to receive. For sheer thrill, you can't forget that valentine you got back in junior high signed, "Guess who?" You could never be sure—but always hoped —it was from that special person.

One of my favorite memories of Valentine's Day is the one when we were newly married and my often absent-minded husband apparently remembered the occasion at the last moment. We were living in a small studio apartment on Boston's Beacon Street and I was feeling a bit depressed and sure that he had forgotten when I went to answer a knock on the door. There stood a boy from Western Union with a telegram for me with the message, "I love you. Please forever be my Valentine," signed, Gerry.

It really made me laugh and I didn't even mind that since I was the only one home, and because the telegram had been sent COD, I had to pay the boy.

THE WIND WITH NO NAME

September 14, 2003

Hooray! Hurricane Isabel is now history and has missed us here in Rhode Island. I have to admit, though, that I had packed some boxes and bags of irreplaceable items to take with me and made a vague evacuation plan. Not needed, I'm happy to say. Isabel, nonetheless, has kicked up quite a storm of hurricane stories and reminiscences, especially of the "big one" of 1938.

My husband, Gerry, and I were here in Rhode Island, young actors just married that year and living with my parents and grandparents. They occupied the second-floor apartment of a two-family Victorian house on a pleasant tree-lined street. The rental included a large room with a turret on the third floor where Gerry and I were temporarily ensconced waiting for a call from our agent in New York.

Sept. 21 was my grandfather's 83rd birthday. Pa, as we called him, was an invalid, and we had planned a small celebration, just some presents and a cake for later in the day, having no way of knowing what was on nature's agenda.

Sometime after lunch, Gerry and I decided to wash the tall windows in our living quarters. The weather, which had been overcast and oppressive, had changed and a stiff breeze began to blow. "Boy!" Gerry remarked, sitting on the windowsill to wash the outside of the glass. "It sure is windy today." Swing music by Tommy Dorsey's band was playing on our radio, and I was singing along with it as I washed the inside glass when I suddenly saw an incredible sight. A large maple tree across the street bent and slowly toppled over into the road as though pushed by a giant hand. Both of us stared. Gerry got off the sill and closed the window.

The wind was now a steady gale. As we stared, another tree, a large oak, crashed to the street, its huge root system taking with it part of the cement sidewalk. Mother came rushing up the stairs to our room.

"Did you see it?" she cried. "What's happening?"

Just then, the music stopped and a radio voice announced that a tropical disturbance was headed our way. The radio crackled and went dead. Mother was worried about Dad, a salesman, who was out in his car.

"He should have been home by now," she said. "Where can he be?"

Suddenly, a side window blew in, showering glass over the room. We pushed the tall desk up against the opening. The turret shook and the whole house seemed to sway.

We rushed downstairs where Pa and Grandma seemed to be a lot calmer than we were.

"What's goin' on?" Grandma asked.

"The radio called it a tropical disturbance," I said. "I think that means a hurricane."

Pa sat in his wheelchair by the window. "Hurricane, my foot!," he scoffed. "Nor'easter. Bad one, maybe," he conceded.

My grandparents had lived a long time and could tell of many disasters. Hurricanes, however, were not a part of their experience. Indeed, the last one to wreck havoc on New England had occurred in 1815, well before living memory.

Looking out at the increasingly ominous scene, we saw a frightening development. The fallen trees had brought down electrical wires, and some of these dangled across the sidewalks and into the street right in the path of children who were coming home from school. We could see a boy and a girl, neighbors, struggling to make their way against the force of the wind. Gerry made a dash for the stairs leading to the ground floor with me close behind him. It was almost impossible to open the front door but we managed to get outside. We tried to shout to the children to go around the wires but the wind blew our voices back to us. Clinging together, we fought our way to the youngsters, helped them get to their nearby home and made it back into our house.

The air was now dense and filled with rain, and objects of all kinds began flying past our second story window. Roof shingles, tree branches, parts of buildings. Outside, the storm was producing an indescribable roar. The atmosphere inside, however, was like a vacuum. Stifling, as though the air had been drawn from the room. The tall building shook and swayed from wind blasts that reached more than 121 mph as we sat there helplessly expecting any moment the upper story of the house would collapse on us.

As bad as it looked, we had no way of knowing the terrible scope of the storm, with winds and the tidal surge that resulted in hundreds of deaths and damage in hundreds of millions of dollars.

After the storm, there were many days without power or phones, no gasoline for cars and food and candles very scarce and expensive.

Still, we were among the lucky ones. Dad arrived safely after midnight after abandoning his car and picking his way through fallen trees back to the house. Pa finally admitted it might have been a hurricane after all, and Gerry got a job working with the cleanup crew, which helped financially while we waited for our big break.

The biggest break for me was getting through the '38 Hurricane and being alive to tell about it all these years later.

PART FOUR

AROUND THE TABLE

VOLUMES WORTH TREASURING

December 5, 2002

Since selling my home a year ago and having lived in several locations since then, I find that the hardest part is having most of my belongings in storage. Of these, by far the most missed items are my books. Not a day passes that I don't long once again to get my hands on them or when I don't look forward to a time when I can set up my bookcases and fill the shelves with them.

It's not that I own a fabulous library of volumes, but what I do have, I prize very highly. Some of them were given to us by my husband's father, a learned man and an Oxford scholar who himself owned a sizeable collection. Mostly, though, what I have is an eclectic mix of works, some in hard cover, some in good shape, a lot in well-thumbed, shabby condition and quite a few common paperback editions. In substance, they cover all kinds of genres from encyclopedia to poetry.

Somehow, when I packed up in a state of confusion and near exhaustion as usual, I grabbed a few random books to take along, hardly noticing what they were and, except for two enormous dictionaries, favoring those volumes that were light and easy to carry. In looking through what now rests on the three small shelves in my very compact work area, I find among them, "Roget's Thesaurus," "Forty Thousand Quotations," a Bible, "Wuthering Heights," "Crime and Punishment" (which I have yet to read), plays by Neil Simon, Arthur Miller and Anton Chekhov, Benjamin Franklin's "Autobiography," books by Isak Dinesen and William Faulkner and an abbreviated volume of Shakespeare, a couple of primers in Spanish and French plus a collection of poetry and several books about writing. Eclectic to say the least, and not much help when it comes to research, I'm afraid.

There are also a few entirely useless paperbacks such as "How to Clean Practically Anything" and "The Blender Cook Book," which would be practical if only I had any idea what has become of my blender.

One item I have handled with utmost care, however. It had remained packed in a box away from the other books until today when, as I began writing this piece, I unwrapped it and gently removed the packing to check it out. It's an old family Bible. Such relics are not really rare here in New England, where many have been cherished and preserved for generations. Mine is not, I fear, in as good condition as I would like it to be, but, it is after all, 266 years old.

While I am not really a genealogy buff, I am able to trace the Bible back nine generations, helped a bit by the recorded dates of births and deaths that were written on a page in between the Old and New Testament sections. Unfortunately, of the covers, only the back remains, the front having been lost years ago.

Most interesting to me is the faded ink-written inscription on the flyleaf. It begins:

"Timothy Locke"

"His Book Bought in the Year 1738

"God Give Him Grace"

Further on is printed:

"The Book of Common Prayer and Administration of the Sacraments and other rites and ceremonies according to the use of The Church of England together with the Psalters or psalms of David Appointed as they are to be sung and said in Churches

"OXFORD

"Printed by John Baskett printer to the University

"MDCCXXXVI"

In doing some quick research to place the age of the book in perspective, I found that in the year 1736, England and its colonies here were under the reign of King George II and the American Revolution was still some 40 years in the future. Benjamin Franklin was 30 years old, George Washington 4 and Thomas Jefferson, so vital in writing the Declaration of Independence, was not yet born. Georgia, the last of the original 13 colonies, had only recently been founded.

There is something unique in looking at and touching, ever so lightly, a volume that has existed and survived in the family over so many years of the country's history.

LETTERS FROM A WHALING SHIP

November 4, 1999

In a recent column, I wrote about attempting to bring order out of chaos by sorting out old letters and papers. I admitted having difficulty in parting with any of these having sentimental connections to my own life. Over the years, however, I have also been custodian of letters from other peoples' lives. People from other centuries, other generations of my family.

When I was still a teenager a great-aunt died and left a box of letters and documents going back to the late 18th century. For years, I carefully carried them with me from home to home, back and forth across the continent, and eventually have placed most of them at the Hay Library at Brown University, where they will be well preserved. I have, of course, kept copies.

My favorites are two letters written by William Remington, third mate of a whaling ship, to his brother Lorenzo, my great-grandfather. William, or Bill, as he refers to himself, had sailed aboard the Covington, out of Warren, Rhode Island. The first letter was sent from the Sandwich Islands (now Hawaii) and dated Nov. 12, 1854. It begins, "Dear Brother, I received your letter one year after it was written, having been in the Post Office eight or nine months." Bill was on a voyage that was to take him over a good part of the Pacific Ocean.

Lahaina, where Bill's ship lay at anchor, was one of the busiest whaling ports in the islands in the 1850s, surpassed only by Honolulu, where it was said that the ships were anchored so close together that you could walk from one end of the harbor to the other on the decks of ships without touching shore.

Apparently, young William had had a falling out with his girlfriend before leaving home and in his letter to his brother; he gets right to the point. "You can tell that I ain't crazy on account of my lovely Fann getting a Bill, so that will make two Bills she has got to my knowledge," he writes. "If that is true, I shall have $500 to spend with somebody else."

Often the whalers would put into the Sandwich Islands and transfer their cargo to a merchant ship, leaving the whaling ship free to make another voyage. They could stock up on fresh meat and vegetables and go ashore to meet friends and enjoy the company of the very friendly native female population amid swaying palms and much festivity. In such surroundings, Bill could afford to be a bit blasé about the fickle Fanny.

"I'm liked in the ship and like very well in return," says Bill in the letter. They apparently had a run of luck and he wasn't shy about taking credit. "We got a thousand barrels this season," he writes. "Me and Mr. Briggs have got the biggest part." As third mate, Bill was in charge of the one of the whaleboats and its crew. When the cry of "Thar she blows" came, it was his duty to help lower the boat and, standing in the bow, direct the oarsmen toward their quarry. "We have been kicked and cuffed about pretty much at every whale we have been onto," he wrote. The sperm whale was a fighter and never gave up easily.

Many a whaler lost his life in that struggle. "We are bound for Hong Kong, the land of silks and camphor trunks," Bill says, "and I wont forget you if I go in the bark. If I leave the bark it will be to get a second mate's berth aboard another ship. There are plenty here where I could go aboard of any day."

William, an early dropout, speaks about returning home and says, "When that will be I don't know for I don't care whether school keeps or not for I have got about learning enough." With a bit of fatalism, he adds, "If I don't live, I make you heir for what is due me." We get a hint of what may have roughed the path of true love when he says, "Tell Fann that she has got a Bill in the good time...for I am steady now. I don't drink a drop, but," he protests, "she was not the cause of my knocking off drinking."

After sending his love and regards to family and friends and asking them to write to him at Lahaina the following June so that he may get them in the fall, Bill ends the letter.

Not, however before he reveals, despite his pretense at indifference, what is really on his mind. "Please to let me know," he says, finally, "if Fanny is married when you write ... and who to."

STANDING THEIR GROUND AGAIN

July 24, 2003

On Sunday, Dec. 19 in the year 1675, an army of 1,000 Englishmen from the vicinity of what is now North Kingstown marched through snow and ice to attack the Narragansett Indian fortress deep in swampland in South Kingstown. The surprise of such a large number of armed Colonists overwhelmed the Narragansetts and resulted in the slaughter of an estimated 600 Indians as well as many women and children.

This massacre undertaken by the Colonists was a preemptive attack. Fearing the Narragansetts might join the Wampanoags under leader King Philip with whom they were waging war, the English struck first. Their only apparent provocation was the refusal of The Narragansett Sachem, Canonchet, to hand over to them a number of Wamponoag refugees. Such captives, Canonchet knew, were sold into slavery in the West Indies if surrendered.

It's been said that Canochet's reply to the demand was, "No. Not a Wampanoag, nor the paring of a Wampanoag's nail."

And now, some 328 years after the Great Swamp Fight, as the event has been named, we once again see the Narragansett Indians standing their ground. This time against State Police officers invading what is left of Narragansett lands with a display of force both unnecessary and embarrassing to many Rhode Islanders. The provocation, in this case, began with the opening of a shop by the Narragansetts selling free tobacco products. A move that led to a swift confrontation with R.I. law enforcement figures.

Of course, there is no comparison between the two events, one that nearly amounted to genocide and the other a clash of views that constitutes state and federal law and the question of sovereignty with a minimum of physical injury. Still, the issues of right and wrong are at stake.

We in America, despite our pride in our country, carry two burdens of guilt, the enslavement of Africans and the gross land theft and the mistreatment of the Indians over several centuries. Both ethnic groups have sought reparation, some has been given, mostly in various types of preferential status in education and job availability. In the case of American Indians, however, the struggle has been to hold their land in sovereign status, which affords them the rights to freedoms of a separate nation within the United States. A resolution of this matter has never been clearly made and has led to debates and confrontations by many Indian tribes and the government over the years.

In Rhode Island, the Narragansetts have been trying to establish some kind of revenue-producing activity, either on their 1,800 acres in Charlestown or in some other area. The first attempt was to obtain permission to operate a bingo parlor, a move that met with opposition from local residents. Following the enormous success of the huge gaming casino the Pequots opened in Connecticut, the Narragansetts set their goal of running a similar money-maker in this state, thereby beginning a seemingly endless series of proposals.

The closest the tribe has come to making the dream come true was in 1994 during the governorship of Bruce Sundlun, who met with the Narragansetts to build a casino in West Greenwich, subject to state referendum. However, in the fall election that year the plan was rejected. The recent fracas between the tribe and the State Police is the result of the Indians' latest attempt to achieve parity and is sure to mark the beginning of extended court action.

Ultimately, the all-important issue of sovereignty will have to be settled at the highest legal level for all Indians, not just the tribes by tribes it would appear. Being among those who are not supporters of smoking or gambling, whether a casino or dog racing, I would still prefer to see a smoke shop than another Foxwoods anywhere in Rhode Island.

In my opinion and that of many others, we already have an overflow of venues where folks are free to lose their paychecks, their social security income, their rent money, and make damn fools of themselves.

EVERYONE DESERVES
EQUAL TREATMENT

March 25, 2004

Like the song says, "the winds of March that make my heart a dancer" are beginning to sweep away the remnants of a hard winter. The tips of bulbs are emerging from the earth and the buds of tree leaves are swelling. One of these days real soon, we can really take a deep breath and sing out, "Spring is here!"

There are other new things springing up besides the change in seasons. One of those is a hot-potato issue, the great demand for legal marriage between gay couples. This is an issue that must be addressed, but which is going to play a much too important role in this election year. No candidate will be able to sashay around it without taking a stand, and opposition to it will be a safe and surefire way for some politicians to curry favor with the far-right groups.

What bothers me most about the controversy is not that there are human beings, couples who love one another and want to share their lives in a legal and conventional type of union. Couples who happen to be of the same gender, but that there are those who believe they have the right to deny these couple their right to the pursuit of happiness, as promised by the Declaration of Independence. And that we have a man holding the highest position in our country who, with his profound bias as well as political motivation, would attempt to attach an amendment to the Constitution banning gay marriage.

The argument most often heard against making gay marriage legal comes from religious opposition. Protestors quote biblical passages and claim that homosexuality is against God's law. That it is unholy, it's sinful. Where do they get their divine authority?

In this country, we live under laws mandated by the Constitution of the United States, not from the Bible, the Torah, the Koran, or any other book. Every religion has its revered prophets and its Holy Writ. And freedom to choose which religion, or none, to follow is guaranteed.

Another opposition to giving devoted gay couples their rights is even harder to understand: the idea that somehow it threatens or diminishes the time-honored status of marriage enjoyed by heterosexuals. People are people and as such, they should have the same privileges.

Homosexuality has existed since mankind evolved in every era of civilization. Sometimes hidden, sometimes not. Marriage among heterosexuals developed for the protection of the human infant, that most vulnerable of creatures. It was intended to make an unbreakable bond between a man and a woman to ensure the future of our species. With the passage of time, however, it has deteriorated and, sadly today, as many as 50 percent of marriages fail, leaving children divided between parents.

There is also a large population of unmarried parents and single-parent homes with children.

Gay couples also often wish to raise children and have often successfully accomplished this.

These concepts are not easily accepted or endorsed by the heterosexual community, of which I am a member. There is not doubt in my mind that the most desirable and happy example of a home consists of a family made up of a father, a mother, and children, safe and secure. This is the norm, and will continue to endure. Unfortunately, there are also many cases of divorced parents and children living in a divided atmosphere of rancor and bitterness.

This is not an ideal world, and human beings are far from perfect. It would seem that wherever there is love and caring between two people, straight or gay, who wish to make a lifetime commitment, society would be best served by sanctioning their union and ensuring that they receive their civil rights.

CONCEIVING A NEW PARENTHOOD

January 31, 2002

W e're living in a world where rapid developments in technology and science continue to dazzle and amaze, while changes in lifestyles and morality tend to shock and confuse some of us. The most recent of these, the emergence of young women being recruited as egg donors to couples unable to conceive the regular way, is the latest mind-bender.

The old saying, "It's a wise child who knows its own father," may now read, " ... who knows its own mother," since it is now possible for a woman whose eggs are infertile to have a donor egg fertilized with her husband's sperm and implanted in her womb.

This procedure, of course, is quite costly, beginning with the recruitment of very special egg donors, preferably college girls with beauty, brains and excellent health ... and depending on the buyer's preferences, special attributes such as being artistic or athletic or having any other outstanding ability. A big order, but the pay is good. Well-to-do searchers are eager to cough up big bucks for the right egg.

Is it any surprise that around this new bonanza has grown a rather unsavory sub-industry of marketing? Brokers who recruit donors (mostly young female college students who need funds for tuition and other expenses and find ads for donors in their campus newspapers). For some of these, the offered payment, for amounts as high as $50,000, looks too attractive to ignore.

Some restrictions have been recommended in limiting the fee to $5,000; however, with all expenses paid, the young lady is whisked off (often to California) to meet and be interviewed by the egg-buying couple. If chosen, she is put on fertility drugs and then, under anesthesia, her eggs are surgically harvested.

There are, of course, certain risks, perhaps even fatal ones, from this procedure. Not enough, evidently, to dissuade several thousand young women who have already made these bargains without giving too much thought to the future: how the donor may feel in years to come, haunted by the knowledge that somewhere a child with her genes, her face and her voice may live without every knowing that the biological mother exists.

Surely, there is no stronger instinct in humankind than the desire to procreate. It is, after all, the force that keeps alive all the species on earth, including ours. There is probably nothing wrong with satisfying that hunger with whatever means are available and legal.

A woman who bears a child using the donor egg method, can, without parting from the truth, tell the future son or daughter about when she was pregnant. The parents can be lyrical about their joy when the baby was born. The fact that biologically another person was involved need not ever be mentioned. They may, as fully adoptive parents sometimes do, choose to keep it all a secret.

The old wisdom recognizes that the real parent is the one who does the important stuff, the day-to-day caring. She who walks the floor with the colicky baby, who is there through sick days and well days, who listens and understands and always supplies the unconditional love is the real "mother" in every case.

It would be up to the individual parents to decide what level of honesty they wish to uphold. Keeping in mind that not revealing all the facts could mean a rift in their relationship with the child if the truth were someday to come out.

Looking deeply into these new possibilities, which may one day include cloning, opens up a Pandora's box of questions about ethics and what's right and what's wrong. It is entirely possible, for example, that soon a couple might make a choice of sperm and an egg from selected donors (giving new meaning to the phrase "mix and match," have the resulting fertilized egg implanted in the womb of a surrogate and, after nine months, go to a hospital and pick up the new baby. Select family planning; "no sweat" parenthood.

Some of us may be fuddy-duddies who still feel it's better to keep doing things the old-fashioned way, especially when it comes to making babies.

MARTIN LUTHER KING JR.

January 20, 2005

This week we have just celebrated the birthday of an important person in the history of our country, Dr. Martin Luther King Jr. For many of us, it was an occasion to remember the achievements of a man who literally gave his life in pursuing a worthy cause: the civil rights of all Americans, the equality of citizens, the dignity of mankind.

Unfortunately, there are some who don't know, understand or appreciate what this individual did that makes him one of the few Americans who deserve to be so honored along with George Washington and Abraham Lincoln. In fact, to some, the holiday is an anomaly. An annoyance, especially in the corporate world where the occasion is often ignored as far as giving workers a day off is concerned.

There are even those who are not sure who Martin Luther King was. "Oh yeah ... That guy ... Wasn't he the first black baseball player?" No, that was Jackie Robinson, the first Negro signed for the Major Leagues by the Brooklyn Dodgers. "What about Joe Louis?" he was the black heavyweight champion of the world, knocking out Max Shmeling back in the Great Depression days. "Oh, I know ... He's the one who refused to give up his seat on a bus to a white guy." No, that was a courageous lady named Rosa Parks.

I can tell you who Martin Luther King was. I knew before this, of course. But since what happened in the 1960s was such a long time ago, I decided to learn more so I went to the library and took out a book about King's life, "The Autobiography of Martin Luther King Jr.," edited by Clayborne Carson.

When I was growing up in a middle-class WASP environment some years ago, I was aware that there were "colored" people somewhere in the city. I had never actually met one. During my 12 years in the

Cranston public school system, I don't recall ever seeing a black student or teacher. Not because the schools were segregated, but the neighborhood unofficially was. In the southern states, of course, segregation was strictly enforced. Later on in life, I had the opportunity to meet and become friends with people of various racial backgrounds and to learn from them and support their fight for civil rights. Dr. King was one of, and the chief spokesman in, that fight. A clergyman who believed in peaceful demonstrations but was not afraid of confronting injustice, he was jailed many times. A winner of the Nobel Peace Prize, he was a great orator and communicator.

As an example of how democracy can and should be developed in a country, there is no better example than how the American people of different races brought about needed changes with the civil rights movement of the 1960s. After the clashes between racists and black people trying to claim their rights to vote, to be treated equally and become first-class citizens—with activists suffering injury, imprisonment and death throughout the South-the long struggle finally culminated with the signing of the Civil Rights Act of 1964 and the Voting Rights Act of 1965.

One of the unforgettable milestones of the movement leading up to these victories occurred during the March on Washington on Aug. 28, 1963. A crowd of 250,000 people, both black and white, assembled before the Lincoln Memorial to hear Dr. King deliver his "I have a dream" speech, which for many people holds a prominence close to Lincoln's address at Gettysburg. Tragically, Dr. King was assassinated in Memphis, Tennessee, on April 4, 1968.

We should honor Dr. King because he was the revered spearhead of a great advance in our society. Because he inspired black Americans with pride, roused his own people to fight against oppression, made white America take notice and ensure constitutional rights to all citizens.

When it comes to American values, perhaps it might be seen that more important than the self-respect King gave his people was the self-respect he helped restore to his species—the honor he brought back to the human race.

PROUDLY HAILED,
THOUGH POORLY SUNG

February 1, 2001

It has been sung, screeched (by such as Roseanne), faked and generally fumbled by almost everybody for going on two centuries now. I think it's about time to admit the truth. Almost nobody knows all the words to our national anthem, "The Star Spangled Banner." Not only that, the music isn't so hot, either. Irving Berlin's "God Bless America" has much better lyrics and an easier tune to remember. Maybe we should replace the former with the latter, if bringing "God" into it wouldn't offend too many people, that is.

Amid the pomp and patriotic goings-on of the recent inaugural ceremonies, there was a moment that brought a real chuckle to this viewer when following the swearing-in phase, everyone attempted to join in singing the anthem. The camera slyly focused for brief shots on the main personages as each tried to rise to the occasion.

The new president took a courageous shot at it, following in with words just a beat after the lead singer, a U.S. Army master sergeant. Vice President Richard Cheney, however, decided to play it safe by not opening his mouth at any time. Some of the others on the dais and in the crowd looked startled and sheepish and made brave attempts to mumble at least some of the words. And what a mouthful of words they are!

O say can you see ... by the dawn's early light,
What so proudly we hail'd at the twilight's last gleaming?
Whose broad stripes and bright stars, thro the perilous fight,
O'er the ramparts we watched were so gallantly streaming?
And the rocket's red glare, the bombs bursting in air,
Gave proof thro the night that our flag was still there.
O say does that Star Spangled Banner yet wave...
O'er the land of the free ... and the home of the brave?

How many of us know what those words represent? I don't recall receiving a clue in school (admittedly a long time ago), and I used to wonder what the heck it was all about. I vaguely thought it was somehow connected to happenings in the Civil War and written by a man named Francis Scott Key. But, hey, it was our national anthem, and almost nobody could sing it all the way through, anyhow.

It's taken me a long time to finally look it up and find out that Key was a young Washington lawyer, who, during the War of 1812, sailed out to the British fleet in Baltimore harbor to obtain the release of a captured American.

During the night of Sept. 13-14, 1814, the British detained Key, and from their ship he was forced to watch as they bombarded Fort McHenry. Luckily, the fort withstood the attack, and seeing our flag still flying at dawn inspired Key to write the verses on his way ashore in the morning.

The lyrics were published in a local newspaper and were set to music taken from a then-popular English song. The Army and Navy long considered it as our national anthem, and President Woodrow Wilson made it official in 1916.

Since it would presumably take another act of Congress to change it —and I somehow can't see such a move coming out of a mostly conservative administration in the near future—I guess we will have to stay with the rocket's red glare and bombs bursting in air, for a while at least.

I don't really wish to disparage Key's heartfelt words. The three verses in the song were inspiring and appropriate in their time and place in history, and "the land of the free, and the home of the brave" will always remain firmly ingrained in the fabric of American tradition. But I would like to hope that sometime in the future a search or contest for a new anthem might result in a song with music everyone could sing and words everyone could relate to and remember.

My father, salesman John Cheshire Jr., leaves for work in 1954.

TRIBUTE TO ARTHUR MILLER

February 24, 2005

On Feb. 10, 1949, a play called "Death of a Salesman" opened at the Marasco Theater in New York City. Now, 56 years later, the author of that play, Arthur Miller, one of our country's greatest playwrights, has died at age 89.

While his distinguished output of dramas over the years, including "The Crucible," "A View from the Bridge," "All My Sons" and a number of others were all inspiring and great successes throughout the theaters of the world, "Death of a Salesman," remains a hallmark of stirring and thought-provoking drama. Its original production, staged by the famous Elia Kazan and starring Lee J. Cobb, was especially powerful in its ability to touch a common chord among many who are able to relate to the experience of Willie Loman, the main character.

Long ago, I had an opportunity to see this first-hand. I once thought of writing about it in an essay to be called "Arthur Miller Killed My Father," which demands an explanation.

In his autobiography, Miller himself remarks about how a great number of people have, over the years, told him how much the character of Willie Loman reminded them of their father, uncle or a close family member and how affected they were by Willie's feelings of betrayal by his world. Willie was a prototype of Everyman, the guy who was worn out by his efforts to play by the rules, give it his all and, in the end, universally left with just the remainder of a dream.

In the mid-1960s, I saw some of that connection between Lee J. Cobb's portrayal of Willie and my dad as we watched a television broadcast made from the original stage production. In the scene where Willie, a traveling salesman, getting older and needing to work closer to home, pleads with his late employer's son to give him the break he'd been promised, I saw my dad's hand gripping the sofa arm, his concentration total. He became Willie, sitting there in that impersonal office, remembering what he had been – one of the best salesmen in New England – buddy-buddy with plant managers and buyers in all the big textile mills. That was what my dad had been until the mills all began to move south to pay lower wages to the workers and his employers reneged on their promises to take care of him when he retired.

At the age of 74, my dad, twice a widower, came from Rhode Island to live with us in California. Although he enjoyed being around our two teenage boys and made social contacts at senior centers, he was always homesick and missing his friends and familiar seasons and surroundings. Just before we viewed the televised Miller play, Dad had suffered a fairly mild stroke but lost his ability to read. This resulted in being unable to play bridge at the two senior centers where he was president and cut down on his activities considerably.

I could see that he was extremely unhappy and tried my best to help. Then came "Death of a Salesman." My dad was essentially a people person. His customers were men who liked to see him coming into their offices with a genuine, sympathetic, friendly smile and handshake. At the end of the Miller play, at Willie's gravesite, a character says, "Willie was a salesman, and for a salesman, there is no rock bottom for the life. He don't put a bolt to a nut, he don't tell you the law or give you medicine. He's a man way out there in the blue, riding on a smile and a shoeshine. And when they don't smile back … that's the earthquake."

A few months after we saw the play, completely by coincidence, my dad had a heart attack and died. The play had absolutely no connection with his passing. I am grateful, though, that he saw it. Someone, in this case Arthur Miller, a great artist, had expressed in his drama feelings that masses of men (and women) would not have been able to show to the world.

Arthur Miller has said that a play like his would not be able to find production on Broadway under today's conditions. It would be too expensive, not commercial enough, the tickets too costly. The general deplorable situation of the lack of national support for the arts is very distressing. In this great nation, we should be embarrassed by this when throughout the world governments of most leading countries are proud to supply hardy financial support to their artists and their work. At present, our National Endowment for the Arts is pitifully under-funded.

When it comes to thinking about true values, it may be time to remember and nurture those gifted newcomers who can, as Arthur Miller did, speak for us, inspire us and enrich our lives.

CALLING GENOCIDE BY ITS NAME

November 2, 2000

Whoever fights, whoever falls, justice conquers evermore.

—Emerson

One of the hardest lessons we all learn as we grow older is how difficult it often is to accommodate ideals to harsh reality ... to decide between justice and expediency.

An example of this was brought to mind by the U.S. House of Representatives' recently shelving a bill that would label the mass killing of Armenians in Turkey genocide. In that event that took place between 1915 and 1923, more than 112 million Armenian men, women and children were taken and systematically slaughtered by order of the Turkish Ottoman rulers in an attempt to exterminate a nation of people who had existed in the area since the 8th century B.C. Some who escaped managed to make their way to America. Many of their descendants remain determined to keep alive the historical record both as a memorial and as a warning to the world.

The reason for the Congressional shelving of legislation is perhaps understandable in the context of complicated and sensitive international relationships. In the name of justice, what took place those many years ago would certainly qualify as genocide. However, in 2000, it happens that we must rely on using Turkey as an air base to patrol the no-fly zone in Iraq, among other considerations, and Turkey is strongly opposed to the proposed bill. President Clinton sent a letter to House Speaker Dennis Hastert with a warning of possible "far-reaching negative consequences for the United States" if the bill came to a vote ... and the cause was abandoned for now. The Turkish president had called Clinton to express concern over the matter and Mr. Clinton's letter to speaker Hastert cited America's interest in containing Saddam Hussein, as well as working for peace and stability in the Middle East and other matters. This expediency won the day; not because of any one person's choice (I'm sure President Clinton would prefer to see the bill passed) but because of the interdependence of nations.

My personal interest in the Armenian situation goes back to childhood. I was a voracious reader as a kid and, at about age 9, my attention was riveted on a book from our shelves, a thick illustrated volume relating the atrocities perpetrated on the Armenians by the Turks. I would pore over this wide-eyed at drawings picturing mothers vainly trying to shield their babies from the bloodthirsty Ottomans. The text was equally as vivid, and the book made a lifelong impression on me.

By the time I reached sixth or seventh grade, several new pupils had joined our class. We learned that they and their families were Armenian refugees who had escaped the violence in their native land. The newcomers were quick to learn the new language and became outstanding students in a remarkably short time.

Like members of other nationalities, Armenian-Americans have spread out across the land contributing significantly to our culture, especially in agriculture and commerce, as well as in the arts and literature. Here in Rhode Island, we have many people who can trace their roots back to Armenia, and in California, where the proposed legislation originated, there are many more. In my view, justice can best be served by the eventual passage of a bill that recognizes the monstrous evil that took place nearly a century ago by calling it by its rightful name: genocide.

KOSOVO AND LITTLETON

April 27, 1999

The beautiful season has come to New England, the time of life and hope and renewal. The time we all yearn for during the dark days of winter when it sometimes seems that deliverance from gloom is far away, but we know that it will surely come. We have an unspeakable faith that it will.

The arrival of spring this year, however, has also brought two dreadful catastrophes along with it. The horrific "ethnic cleansing" in Kosovo and the student shootings in Littleton, Colo. We may escape the constant coverage of these tragic events by not listening, watching or reading about them for short periods of time, but this is an age of news saturation and keeping informed is almost a way of life.

Those of us who have been around a long time have never expected to see the massive uprooting of people from their homes in Europe again in our lifetimes. Long lines of refugees with babies, bewildered elderly, mothers with little ones clinging to their skirts, stretched across barren fields and roads on their way to unknown destinations, trying to keep alive under inhuman conditions. Hoping against hope to find loved ones among the crowd ... unable to mourn at unmarked graves of those lost and murdered.

On the lips of many of these desperate people (in their language or ours) is the word "home." They want to live, but they are not hoping to be sent to America—or England—or to Australia. What they want most is to return to their villages, to their families and friends. Alas, whatever the fortunes of war, it seems unlikely that this will ever happen.

The fate of these unfortunates was on my mind a great deal as I flew home from my recent visit to California. Back to my snug little house in my friendly, pretty village in South County. I felt safe—as do many others who are lucky enough to live in this country. But there are dangers to that safety, and luck can run out. On April 20, it ran out in Littleton.

Throughout the news media, the endless series of interviews, the "expert" opinions, traumatized students and parents, all are searching for answers—and a place to put the blame for unspeakable tragedy. Does the fault lie with parents? Schools? Movies and TV? Violence in society? Police inadequacy? Failure of government and laws? Gun availability? There is certainly enough blame to go around.

The thing that is so difficult to fathom is, how could so much hatred be generated in the minds and hearts of young people? How could they be so callous to the sacredness of life and the finality of death—including their own? Where did we, the adults, go wrong?

High school is no picnic. The idea of it being a happy, carefree time is a myth. I can remember feelings of humiliation, deep hurt, envy, jealousy, enormous self-consciousness and embarrassment—and I was one of the fairly well-adjusted ones, with a stable home life, plenty of friends, dates and good times. The sting of the bad times, however, is still there.

There were always the ones who didn't fit in, who were "different," the ones we snickered at when they acted a certain way in class and wore clothes we didn't think were cool. Maybe they hated us. Maybe—if times were different—if they had banded together in their disaffection, if weapons were readily available and the recipe for bomb construction was available on a screen at home—who knows—maybe?

One thing is certain. We must reach out to our young people at an early age. Build up their egos, their sense of self-worth. Teach them tolerance for others and confidence in their own abilities. One prominent psychologist has said, "Long before adolescence, we need to be alert to the anger, humiliation and frustration of our children ... and accept expressions of anger at home, tantrums or inappropriate language."

In other words, let them blow off a little steam where it can be tempered with understanding and love. And, above all, keep abreast of what's going on with them, what they're into, who their friends are, how they feel about themselves and others. And still achieve this without smothering them. A tall order.

Now there is a war going on in Europe, and a battle here at home for the hearts and minds of our children. May we find the strength and wisdom to guide them into becoming adults who can recreate a world where problems are not solved with weapons, and killing is not a game.

A MEMORABLE PLACE FOR ALL

June 22, 2002

Home is the place where, if you go there, they have to take you in.

I wish I could remember who said the above ... one of the truly great quotes. And as we collectors of cliché and insightful folk wisdom would say, "They hit the nail right on the head." I am sure that most of us, doing an honest appraisal of the past, can remember a time when the words rang true for ourselves, and later on for our children and their children. I'm referring, of course, to those lucky enough to have some kind of family "net" strong enough to give temporary sanctuary and emotional sustenance through times of trial or transition. Such experiences can strengthen family ties, while testing the limits of one's patience and sense of humor.

Over the years, my husband and I were able to both receive and give that kind of family support. I especially think of the time, just after the end of World War II, when, as a young couple with a three-year-old son, we went to stay for a brief time with my husband's family. Although not in the service, Gerry had worked for a very long time and very long hours in a defense plant and was due for a bit of a rest and change of career. We were invited by his parents to come to Pennsylvania and, as they put it, "take a break." This sounded great and, packing up our belongings, we left our cramped war-time digs in Boston and took off.

When we arrived at the Leaper home in the lush countryside outside Philadelphia, we found we weren't the only ones needing a break. Already staying in the three-story farmhouse were all the members of the family, including Gerry's parents and three comely sisters, including the oldest, a beauty who was getting a divorce and had come home with her toddler. His brother, Joe, an airman recently liberated from two years in a German POW camp, also had been invited to stay there with his wife and three-year-old daughter to "get back on his feet." And now, the three of us. There were in all nine adults and three very young kids. But it was a big house.

In spite of the problems, tensions, misunderstandings and inevitable quarrels that eventually ensued, I remember it as being warm and funny and special. I grew up an only child in a household with four adults, my parents and grandparents, and while I always feel that I had a wonderful childhood, it was a New England kind of wonderful. More stringent, you might say. Certainly not as emotionally charged as my husband's Irish family background. His dad, an Oxford-taught distinguished chemist; his mother, a daughter of Erin who actually kissed the Blarney stone at an early age. His three knockout-pretty sisters with their retinues of suitors at the door at all hours; his brother, almost unrecognizably thin from his prison camp ordeal yet always ready with dry witty commentary on whatever was going on.

I adored my mother-in-law, a short, plump lady with an infectious laugh who was full of tales of her native Ireland. The last of 12 children, she came to America at age 17 to join her older brothers. She bid her elderly parents farewell and, sadly, never saw them again. She had a gift for attracting all sorts of people who enjoyed her company. Life around her was never dull. She often mislaid her purse and her cry would echo through the house, "I've lost my pocketbook! Don't anybody move until I find it!" We would all stay still as statues until the mystery was solved.

You never knew what to expect. One day, dressed to go out in one of her "slimming" print dresses, with lots of matching jewelry, she first went out to the poultry house, wrung the necks of a couple of chickens and brought the carcasses into the kitchen.

"Here," she commanded, "you girls pluck and clean these and I'll cook them for dinner when I get back."

My father-in-law, equally unpredictable, was a scholar, a product of English high education who was well versed in classical poetry, Shakespeare, and the lyrics of Gilbert and Sullivan operettas. He took delight in buttonholing any one of his daughters' boyfriends in the parlor with a discussion of one of these subjects interspersed with double talk that left the poor fellow both baffled and terrified.

When we left that household for quieter digs of our own, I found myself missing the confusion, the humor, and, most of all, the warmth of being part of a large family where I was always made to feel that I belonged.

PART FIVE

A MOVEABLE FEAST

WESTWARD HO!

January 11, 2001

The conclusion of World War II was the end of an era, and for many people was a time for new beginnings. After the tensions, long working hours, and uncertainties of the 1940s, we decided to take the big leap of moving to California with our little family, which now included our two boys, Gerry Jr., (called Roddy), age 9, and Jeff, 5.

The year was 1951. Gerry and I were now in our 30's, and we mulled over the possibilities of returning to New York where we had met, and trying our luck in the newly emerging television industry, or going to Los Angeles where friends had already relocated and sent letters of praise about opportunities there. Eventually, on this encouraging note, full of the spirit of adventure, and quite a bit of naïveté, we packed up our two small boys and drove a 1946 Chevy hauling a utility trailer loaded with household goods to California. The result could have been disaster. In truth, however, we had more good luck than bad. And ended up living there for more than three decades.

The road we took was the famous old Route 66, which for 75 years was the motor trail for those traveling west across the country. From the days of the Dustbowl and Steinbeck's "Grapes of Wrath," which depicted the plight of those fleeing the deserted farms to decades later when it was made obsolete by a modern highway, Route 66 was the way to reach "California or Bust." It has become such an icon of nostalgia that books, magazines and many articles have been written about it. Its many aficionados were delighted to hear that the Smithsonian Institution was digging up a portion of the old road to add to a new transportation exhibit, which was finally to open in 2003.

With the loaded trailer ready to start the trip in September of 1951

ROUTE 66

Reading about the Smithsonian Institution's transportation exhibit led me to my original journal, which I began keeping in early 1950.

I found preserved a day-to-day account of that trip we made the following year. While there were many trials, car troubles and stops to rearrange the load, which we encountered before arriving in Los Angeles, I'll leave the details described in the journal, which I hope will be of some interest to future generations and only include a few excerpts here.

Monday, Oct. 29: Having left Rhode Island, visiting and saying goodbye to family members in Philadelphia, we hit the turnpike and began the trip west today.

Tuesday, Oct. 30: Springfield, Ohio ... We hit the Pennsylvania Turnpike around 2:30 yesterday and spent the night at a motel in Somerset, Pennsylvania. After a bit of car trouble in the morning, we traveled to Pittsburgh and reached Springfield, Ohio, late this afternoon.

Wednesday, Oct. 31: Decatur, Illinois ... We rode through a lot of farmland and flat prairie today.

The weather has been cold and overcast. It snowed for a little while. We saw a bit of Indiana. It is Halloween night but the kids don't seem to mind missing the Trick or Treat too much this one time. We've promised that next year we will really celebrate.

Had a good dinner here in Decatur at a restaurant up the road from the motel and are going to bed early.

Thursday, Nov. 1: Rolla, Missouri ... We rolled into St. Louis around noon today and ate lunch in Forest Park, one of the three largest in the country. Got a peek at their outdoor theater and the Jewel Box, a kind of inside botanical garden. We pushed on hoping to get some distance but were overtaken by snow. This is in the Ozarks and very pretty, if lonely, country.

Friday, Nov. 2: Claremore, Oklahoma ... we stayed tonight in Will Roger's hometown and at the hotel named in his honor. It is comfortable and quiet and we had T-bone steaks for $2 apiece for dinner. Must have each weighed a pound and a half ... saw some cowboys.

Saturday, Nov. 3: Amarillo, Texas ... We went through Tulsa and Oklahoma City, a bright progressive town. We ate lunch at a swanky place called Beverly's ... and us all looking like Okies. Everybody here in Amarillo looks like they may be wealthy. We are staying at the Hillcrest Court where we have a suite...2 bedrooms and 2 baths for $7 ... and everything beautiful. I could stay here for a week!

Sunday, Nov. 4: Grants, New Mexico ... we reluctantly left Amarillo and drove through prairie, hot and windy, to Albuquerque. Saw Indians and Mexicans, all with stuff for sale.

We stopped for gas and went inside a stockade where there was a caged coyote and two fiercely growling wildcats ... both clutching bloody hunks of jack rabbit. The kids got quite a kick out of it.

Monday, Nov. 5: Holbrook, Arizona ... Today, we reached Gallup, New Mexico, which is the headquarters of the Indian Affairs Bureau. The railroad has an employment office there. The town is teeming with Indians ... squaws in blankets with babies and little kids and long-haired men in pony tails under big hats. A short distance from town we saw a long train stopped with flames and smoke coming from one of the cars. A crowd of Indians stood by ineffectually trying to douse it with pails of water. We stopped and took a picture. A bit later, at a place called Navajo, our car ran off the road into a culvert and was hung up with one wheel dangling over the edge. Finally, Gerry located a truck to haul us out and we drove here to a motel in Holbrook.

Tuesday, Nov 6: Kingman, Arizona ... Today we proceeded on our way to the Grand Canyon. I wanted to see the Painted Desert but the car trouble held us up and it was dark by the time we were in the area. Gerry handed me the flashlight to look out the window, but of course it was useless ... Thank Goodness, today we did get to see the Canyon, however. Climbing the winding hills caused us some worry about the car pulling the loaded trailer behind us, but we made jokes and were enthralled with the changing terrain, which often looked like another planet with sparse vegetation and queer rock formations. Finally, we got to the Grand Canyon Forest and *burst on to the Desert View Observatory. The view was beautiful, awesome and very, very still. Looking down, it is timeless, immense, beautiful and horrible ... a foretaste of heaven or hell. I am grateful that all of us had the opportunity to experience it. After leaving the Canyon, we drove back through lovely country to Kingman and a motel.*

Wednesday, Nov. 7: Los Angeles, California ... Tonight we arrived in L.A. after driving all day through the desert and then through orange country and mountains and saw the smog of Southern California. The sun set in a haze so that it looked like an orange ball surrounded by smoke. We finally reached Burbank, are staying at a motel and will begin looking for a place to rent.

The weather is grand, and the houses all look so pretty and there are flowers everywhere.

Discovering the University of California at Los Angeles during 1954.

Picking wildflowers with the boys in the Sierra Mountains.

DUTCH

October 28, 1999

When Edmund Morris's book about Ronald Reagan, entitled "Dutch," made its debut in 1999, it brought back memories of living in Hollywood the first two years after we arrived in California. In the previous chapter, I told about the journey Gerry and I and our young sons made to the West Coast in 1951, which finally brought us to Burbank, close by the fabled land of Hollywood.

When we set out on the journey, we had a few hundred dollars in cash and a promise of a job for Gerry at Lockheed in Burbank. However, besides having mastered the trade of tool-and-die maker, Gerry was also experienced in theater and had ideas about somehow working his way into the movie studios. The word was, of course, that it was impossible without "pull" from someone in the industry. All studio jobs were under the iron control of studio workers unions, we were told, and he was advised to forget about it.

We settled in to stay with friends while we searched for our own place and the second day there, Gerry confidently picked up the phone and called RKO Studios in Hollywood and described his technical background. He was told that they did have an opening in the camera department, directed him where to go to join the union IATSE (International Alliance of Theatrical Stage Employees) and very shortly he was, indeed, a Hollywood movie picture studio employee. Bye-bye, Lockheed.

Our next break was solving the problem of living quarters. I had made up my mind to look for something different. After all, if you're going to live in a glamorous town, I reasoned, why look for the mundane? Even without much money. I guess the fairy godmother of all innocents was watching over us; because when I answered an ad for a house in the Hollywood Hills, we hit the jackpot. Climbing four sets of steps (100 in all) with interesting dwellings at each level and fragrant flower shrubs growing along the paths, we finally arrived at a Spanish-style house with a 40-foot living room, a fireplace, two bedrooms with French doors to the patio and a small kitchen and bath. We got all this for $90 a month! It was also partly furnished, which, along with the things we had brought with us, made it look homey, but still glamorous.

Our landlady, who lived next door, was a former movie "dress extra," one who appeared in scenes that called for large groups of people in evening dress. She was an interesting and warm-hearted person and had many stories to tell about the old movie days. Both her sons were cinematographers. One of them, at that time, head camera-man for the "I Love Lucy" television show.

All around our house, located just above the Hollywood Bowl, lived people connected to the movie business: actors, writers, designers, technicians. It was here that we met Judy, the sister of a neighbor. Judy was blonde, vivacious, and an actress and singer, then appearing at Ciro's, the famed nightclub on the Sunset Strip. We were invited to see the show and, while there, were introduced to some celebrities, including the famous Hollywood gossip columnist, Louella Parsons. A few months later, we were happy to offer Judy and her fiancé and their guests, our living-room, in which the couple exchanged wedding vows, presided over by a family friend, a judge.

Judy had some interesting tales to tell, which included her stories about former boyfriend, Ronald Reagan. As described by Judy, he was a nice guy but talked far too much. Yackety-yack … all about current events and politics and such, which to her were less than fascinating subjects. He also, she complained, had a very dominating mother. Judy apparently had stopped seeing Ronnie because of these "faults." and neither she nor anybody else had a hint of his fabulous future.

Years later, when we had moved from Hollywood to the San Fernando Valley, Reagan became a Republican, championing right-wing causes. During his tenure as California governor he cut funds to welfare, medical services and aid to education. His callous attitude toward environmental issues ("When you've seen one redwood you've seen them all") also did not endear him to a lot of people. However, in 1980, as we all know, he was elected to the country's highest post, served for two terms and deserves credit for a number of achievements.

As to the Morris book, despite some over-done passages and the confusing use of the author as fictional Reagan contemporary, it appears to be a thorough and valuable work. It is also colorful enough to reawaken interest in what it takes to reach that peak of power, president of the United States.

MEMORIES OF A MENAGERIE

May 4, 2000

My nearest neighbors have acquired baby animals in the spirit of springtime. On one side, there is a new calf, and on the other, a Newfoundland puppy. Makes me think back a few years when my husband and I and our two boys lived in our first home in California's San Fernando Valley.

We bought a small house on three-quarters of an acre, which had about half that area planted to fruit trees. Five-year-old trees just coming into bloom … enough, in that time and place, to be considered a small ranch. There were also some out buildings. The boys slept in one of these, which we fancifully named the Bunkhouse. Somewhat primitive, but an adventure for them.

Soon after we moved in, we began to acquire our menagerie. First came Tyler, a beautiful purebred collie who closely resembled Lassie (who was really a male). He came to us from owners who didn't have the necessary space needed for a big dog. Then there were several cats, and eventually kittens. Someone also gave us a duck named Dillard, which, of course, necessitated the construction of a small pool for him to paddle around in. Dillard provided lots of fun when we introduced a rubber duck into his watering hole. Dillard accepted the fake bird but was devastated when it sprung a leak and began sinking. He made heroic attempts to rescue the ersatz fowl, diving down, grasping the rubber neck in his bill and bringing it to the surface … only to have it sink again. Finally, we took pity on Dillard and spirited the "body" out of his sight.

Eventually we became owners of more ducks and a pair of geese who woke us every morning just after sunrise by coming up to the back patio and quacking loudly for breakfast.

It wasn't long before we found out that Dillard was really a duck and

Tyler and Bugs Bunny.

Dillard and friends enjoy the pond.

not a drake, as we had supposed, when he/she laid a large white egg. Since there was an existing poultry house, we also got some chickens and a rooster. With spring in the air, our Rhode Island Red took to disappearing into the thick ivy surrounding a birdbath—and one day emerged proudly leading a half-dozen baby chicks.

At some point, the boys became owners of two rabbits, which were in separate cages and as far as anyone knew, were on strictly platonic terms. There had been a rumor, however, that a wild rabbit had been seen around the cages, and one night the boys came running in to announce that baby bunnies were being born in one of them. A mystery! But after all, it was spring—and they were rabbits.

Technically, the boys were supposed to feed all the animals before leaving for school, but somehow there never was enough time. Consequently, I found myself leaving the house around 9 each morning armed with carrots, lettuce, duck pellets, cheese, cracked corn and whatever else I could find. Slowly, I proceeded from one enclosure to another dispensing nourishment.

There was suspense involved in my travels as from time to time various pets had escaped, and walking through the tall grass by the rabbit cages, I couldn't help wondering what had happened to that large alligator lizard. Not to mention the free, roaming gopher snake and a big black and white rat.

Our place seemed to be a magnet for wildlife, and soon a beautiful male pheasant flew off course and made a landing in our orchard. He took a shine to the ducks and chickens and stayed around for free grub for quite a while.

Looking back at the experience and my role as "Mrs. Noah," I remember that the chores were sometimes tiring, but I wouldn't have missed it for the world.

The boys showing off in the orchard.

Kittens play in the yard.

TIME TO HIT THE ROAD...AGAIN

June 28, 2007

Let's take a boat to Bermuda,
Let's hop a bus to St. Paul.
Let's take a powder to Boston for chowder,
Let's get away from it all.

—Old popular song

Vacation time is upon us, and many folks are heading for the beach or the mountains or perhaps planning a camping trip. I was reminded of this recently while leafing through one of my many albums of snapshots taken when the family was growing up. Memories flooded back of outings we made ... some great, a few, not so hot.

Let's face it. Some people are cut out for camping and roughing it in the wilds ... and others are not. Now, I love the great outdoors and the marvels of nature. I have read John Muir and Henry David Thoreau and even lived near Walden Pond (before they "cleaned" it up). The only trouble is, when night comes on I start thinking about comfortable motels with soft beds and hot showers. There's something about the smell of wood smoke and tent canvas that sets my pulses racing and fills me with a desire to jump in the car and head for the nearest Hilton.

Of special memory is one trip we made with friends when our kids were young. It was planned for just one or two nights. There were ten of us all together, six boys and four adults. And we had agreed to keep it simple, only the barest necessities. This included two tents, a collection of borrowed sleeping bags and air mattresses, cooking equipment, food, clothing and fishing gear for 10 people. It came to slightly less baggage than that carried by the British Mount Everest expedition.

We got off to a fairly early start, around 9, which wasn't too bad considering we had planned to leave at 7. Somehow, it seemed like a bad omen when upon backing out of the driveway, we ran over one of our boy's bikes. This led to a spirited discussion over whose fault it was ... who left the bike there, etc. Nevertheless, we finally managed to get on the road.

The ride was comparatively uneventful, involving only five stops for coffee, restrooms and gasoline and several stops to wait for our friends, who took the wrong turn and had to come back.

We arrived at the lake about noon and were assigned two adjoining campsites. Filled with enthusiasm, the boys poured from the two cars and began unpacking. Before you could say, "I was a teenage nut," the tents were up and all the gear strewn tastefully over the landscape.

We women prepared a picnic lunch on the camp table and got a fire going for coffee. It was during this period that it began to dawn on us that, to put it mildly, we had been given an undesirable location. We were in an exposed, windy area with nothing but dust underfoot, and on a corner where every passing car threw up a cloud of the stuff to settle on our food, table, and in our faces. True, we had been told we could pick out another spot if we were weren't satisfied, but the tents were all up and the boys were eager to be off fishing.

Well, nobody caught any fish. Back they all came, tired and hungry at suppertime. Little Phillip got a fishhook in his finger, little Peter had fallen in the water, Jeff got into some poison oak, and Mickey had stepped on a broken bottle.

While the fathers hastily set up an emergency field hospital, we mothers started once again the laborious meal preparations. Several hours later, soot-blackened, dust-laden, and exhausted, we sat and looked at one at one another. Somebody, I think it was I, spoke those immortal words, "Let's hit the road!"

This cry seemed to strike a common chord, for no sooner was it uttered then baggage started to be loaded back into the cars faster than it had been unpacked.

It's true that there were a few dissenting voices raised among the small fry, but these were quickly silenced with a kindly, "Be quiet and GET BACK IN THE CAR!"

We made it home in record time.

In spite of the hardships of the day, I looked upon it as a valuable experience.

Because of it, home never looked so good, beds were never so comfortable, and the next morning I went out to the kitchen, threw my arms around my electric stove and gave it a great big kiss!

Note: In case you're wondering about the kids, I'm happy to report that later on that summer we went on some really fun-filled excursions. And I've got pictures to prove it!

A GOOD NEIGHBOR

July 16, 1998

*A more important thing
than fame,
Is the way you play
the game.*

It appears to me that one of the most necessary components of a satisfying life is having a sense of community. Of feeling at home in a neighborhood and relating to people and mutual issues in a positive way. I was reminded of this by the recent death of Roy Rogers, known to millions as "King of the Cowboys." To those of us who lived in the town of Chatsworth, California, in the 1960s, however, the Rogers family members were part of the community.

My husband and I and our two sons moved to the town in the late 1950s. Situated in the northwest corner of the San Fernando Valley, part of the City of Los Angeles, Chatsworth was still a sleepy western town of ranches and orange groves where many celebrities had homes, escaping the pressure of Hollywood and Beverly Hills. Fred Astaire kept horses there on his ranch. Barbara Stanwyck had a home there and Lucy and Desi had just moved away. Famed novelist Ayn Rand, author of "The Fountainhead," wrote in her Chatsworth home. Actor Dan Daily and TV stars Chad Everett and James Brolin (who married Barbra Streisand) lived there.

Roy and Dale and their brood of nine kids lived in a sprawling ranch house on acreage with plenty of room for their horses.

We bought a small house and guest house on two acres a few miles from the Rogers home. Part of what had been a large ranch now divided into parcels, our place had grapes, orange and lemon trees, olives, peaches, as well as some pine and eucalyptus and a variety of exotic, as well as native, plants and flowers. We had two collie dogs, a number of cats and a burro named Sally. Behind our hill, open chaparral-covered land stretched for miles, providing the background for many scenes filmed for movies and TV. Our boys loved roaming the hills where there were deer, bobcats and even an occasional mountain lion. Not far away was the old run-down Spahn Movie Ranch, later to become infamous as the headquarters of the "Manson Family."

As the permissive movement of the 60s began to spread, Chatsworth became an odd mixture of long-haired hippies and strong conservatives. The latter were perhaps personified by Roy and Dale and their family. Roy served as "Honorary Mayor" of Chatsworth, a position that only required him to ride his horse in parades and make a speech or two at local events. When he was available, however, he was obliging and always down to earth. He was often seen at the local skeet-shooting range, a spot also visited by Clark Gable and other notables.

Despite their fame, the Rogers tried to live their lives as ordinary folk. They raised their family: Roy's three kids from his first marriage (his wife died after childbirth), Dale's son, four adopted children, and one foster child, with their idea of American values. Sadly, the only child born to Roy and Dale, a little girl with Down Syndrome, died at age two. They were members of a small local church and suffered another tragedy when another daughter was killed in a bus accident while on a church outing.

Both Roy and Dale could be counted on when it came to community affairs. Our son Jeff belonged to a church youth group whose members were invited to the Rogers' home. They were entertained by Roy, who took them through the house, ending up in his den and trophy room, where he proceeded to set up a movie projector and show the youngsters footage of his hunting trips to Africa and Alaska. Refreshments were also served. It was a memorable experience for all.

The Rogers' oldest boy, Roy Jr., known as Dusty, graduated from high school in the same class as our son. That year, my husband and I wrote and produced a variety show as members of the school's parent group. We were not personal friends of the Rogers, but I had a nodding acquaintance with Dale since we both went to the same hairdresser and I had sat under the dryer next to her several times. We decided to ask her to take part in the show and she graciously accepted, saying she would bring her own music. Sure enough, on performance night, like the pro she was, Dale showed up and sang several songs, accompanying herself on piano.

Roy and Dale were celebrities. But more than that, they were good people, fine neighbors and a credit to the community.

LITTLE SOUNDS
MAGNIFIED BY NIGHT

March 9, 2000

Today it seems as though spring has arrived. Bulbs are coming up fast, robins have shown up and the earth is mostly frost-free. From past experience, however, we long-time New Englanders know that March, while seductive, can be just a tease.

Looking through my diaries of the past few years, I see that anything from snowstorms to nor'easters can arrive during both March and April, and although I can't restrain the urge to plant seeds in containers, I'm not ready to store away the winter clothing—or the snow shovel—yet.

To those of us light sleepers who sometimes lie awake midway through the long January and February nights, the arrival of early daylight is welcome. Lying awake has, however, made me conscious of night sounds. My old house provides a whole program, making me aware that I am far from alone.

There's the running, scuffling patter of little paws above my bedroom ceiling, during which I imagine a family of squirrels cavorting in the attic, followed by the occasional scraping or gnawing sounds, which can come from anywhere. Vaguely alarmed, I sometimes get up from bed and pound on the wall where I think the perpetrators might be. This seems to get through to them, until a short time later when the sounds come from another direction.

Then there's the noise that comes from hot water being heated up by the oil burner into the baseboard units. Thumps, cracking, a whole repertoire of sounds, rather comforting to the initiated during a frosty night, but disturbing to a visiting granddaughter who hadn't been told what to expect and spent the first night without much sleep. She was charmed in the morning, however, to hear the lowing of cows from next door. City people, I find, like country sounds.

I remember the first night I ever spent in New York City. As a young girl coming from a quiet suburb the honking horns, constant wails of sirens and motors of heavy traffic all blended into a cacophony that made sleep elusive or impossible. It wasn't too long, however, before I became accustomed to the racket and could adjust, which isn't all that hard to do when you're 19.

The sounds of the night differ with the location. Here in the Ocean State, at one time or another, many of us have been lulled to sleep by the rhythm and music of breaking ocean waves with the repeated sounds of a foghorn adding a touch of mystery. The sort of bedtime song that can lead to dreams of adventures and far-away places.

Living in Southern California had its own brand of night magic. Here in the East, apart from the chorus of peepers in the pond and per-haps a hoot from an owl, we seldom hear much from wildlife after dark. In the West, the night brings the howl of coyotes calling (sometimes here, too, nowadays), foxes barking and that tireless songster, the mock-ingbird.

Near our home up against the rocky hills of Chatsworth, a mocking-bird and his mate had a nest high up in a Monterey pine and he began disturbing my rest in late April and continuing well on into May. I first became conscious of him when his clear, liquid notes started waking me every night around 1 a.m. I struggled up from sleep and lay listening to his ever-changing song, first with annoyance and then with grudging admiration. After a while, I would usually drift off while he was still warbling but one night, unable to sleep, I got up, threw on my robe and slippers and went outside.

The moment I stepped out onto the porch I was entranced. Moonlight illuminated the entire landscape. The porch with its white railing was like the deck of a ship riding high above the field below, dot-ted with grapevines and oak trees and with a row of pines on the left. Upon the topmost branch of the tallest tree perched the mockingbird, clearly outlined against the sky. I'm sure he saw me there but gracious-ly accepted my intrusion and continued to pour forth cadence after cadence of song. Never once did he repeat himself.

I stood there for a long time and he was still trilling when I went back inside. Gone was my annoyance. I drifted off to sleep very grate-ful for the experience and the lovely concert.

THE TREASURE
OF STARLIGHT HILL

May 3, 2001

The introduction to the public of the R.I. state quarter, the 13th in the U.S. Mint's 50 States Quarters Program, took place recently in Newport with a number of VIPs, including Governor Almond, Congressmen Patrick Kennedy, James Langevin and others in attendance.

It may still be a couple of weeks before the historical coins that, on the back, show a typical bay scene of a yacht in full sail, will be available from local banks. Each of the 50 state quarters are made for only ten weeks and will never be produced again (I wish I had known that earlier; I've let a whole lot of those other state quarters slip through my fingers, thinking they would keep on coming).

Coins have always been a source of interest to a lot of people, as well as a basis for stories. Stories about a "lucky coin" or a "magic coin" or even a "bewitched coin." I can't vouch for any of those, but I do have a 100 percent true tale about coins that took place when we were living in California.

It began one day when my husband, Gerry, entered the basement of our home and selected a 6-foot length of pipe and a wrench. He had just returned from an inspection tour of Starlight Hill, the fancy name we'd given our two rocky acres, and had found a section of the sprinkling system that needed repairing. Tools in hand, he made his way up the hill, noticing, as he went, that the pipe he carried was extremely heavy. Both ends, he realized, were covered with screw-on caps.

It would be a problem if he couldn't remove the caps. He stopped midway up the path and applied the wrench to one end.

As the cap came off, something small and shiny fell out and rolled on the ground at Gerry's feet ... a dime. Mystified, he shook the pipe gently. It made a clinking sound. Excited now, but still unbelieving, he dropped the wrench and made his way down the hill to the cellar. He took an empty carton from the shelf and up-ended the pipe into it.

A river of dimes poured into the box! Some shiny, some dull, but all of them beautiful. Gerry ran his hand through the coins. Then he remembered that there had been another pipe.

Up in the house, the boys and I heard him calling us, and we ran down to see what was going on. When I got there, I found the boys bending over the cardboard carton, staring at the box of dimes in disbelief. Gerry was at the workbench holding a long pipe, one end of which was in his bench vise while he worked to remove the cap from it.

"This one's larger around than the other," Gerry said. "I can't seem to get this cap off, though."

"Do you think it's full of more dimes?" Jeff asked, excitedly.

"Maybe it's quarters," Rod said.

"We'll soon find out," Gerry said, and with a final effort, he managed to remove the cap. He carried the pipe over to a second box and tilted it towards the floor. Out came another flood – a beautiful clanging stream.

"Oh boy," shouted our sons. "Half dollars!"

"Hundreds of them," Jeff shouted. "Buried treasure!"

"How long do you think they've been there, Dad?" Rod asked, when we had all quieted down a bit.

"It must've been quite a while," Gerry said. "None of them seem to be dated later than 1941."

"Here's one that says 1878," Jeff said. "And 1916, 1900 ... "

As soon as we got a hold of a coin catalogue, we discovered that many of them were collector's items, a fact that added greatly to their value. Of course, we wondered how the coins came to be there and who had stored them in the pipes. We knew the property had changed hands several times before we bought it. When we told the story to a group of friends, the most interested listener was our next-door neighbor who had sold us the place. At the end of the tale he shook his head.

"So that's what it was," he sighed. "You know, right after I bought the property I took a whole load of those heavy pipes to the dump. Don't know how I missed those two. I thought they were filled with cement."

"WHAT DUMP?" we all chimed in chorus.

Our neighbor smiled sadly. "The one they filled in two years ago," he said.

Later we took a ride past the former dump. A modern complex of apartments now occupied the site.

"Just think," Jeff said as we rode by. "Those people don't even know that they're living right on top of the treasure of Starlight Hill!"

POTLUCK

June 28, 2001

On June 21, 2007, an Associated Press article stated that the Rhode Island Medical Marijuana Bill, set to expire June 30, had been made permanent, Governor Donald Carcieri's veto having been overridden by the state legislature. It allows patients with cancer, AIDS and other debilitating illnesses to possess up to 12 marijuana plants and two-and-a-half usable ounces of the drug. The announcement brought back a certain personal event in my life in the 1960s … a time when anything could happen. And often did.

It started out innocently enough when someone gave me some seeds. He told me they were mystery seeds. He said they were special. Plant them, he said, you'll see.

Did I know what I was doing? After all, I was a grown-up. Did I guess? Maybe I didn't want to know. Anyhow, I planted the seeds … all 15 of them. In pots in my plant shelter in California.

It was around that time when Charles Manson and his "family" lived over the hill from us at Spahn's old cowboy-movie ranch and were frequently seen on their "garbage runs," picking up discarded produce behind the markets in Chatsworth.

It was around that time that our car along with others got pulled over on the outskirts of Santa Barbara while gun-toting police surrounded a van they suspected might be carrying the kidnapped heiress, Patty Hearst, then being sought for bank robbery.

It was also the season when Franciscan monks in their long brown robes stood in the center divider of California Route101 at Santa Barbara passing out leaflets urging the boycott of white grapes in support of labor leader Caesar Chavez, and the migrant workers … and when my husband and I joined other marchers in protesting the war in Vietnam.

We had tried smoking grass a few times, too. Didn't like it and quit. We were a bit out of sync, you might say. Too square to be hippies, and too hip to be yuppies.

So I shouldn't have been surprised to see what came up from those seeds I planted. Every one of them sprouted, sending up strong slender stems with long thin-notched leaflets. Beautiful green lush foliage.

I'll admit I was thrilled. I am, after all, a plant nut. One who grows anything that will sprout, transplant, or root. Who does not discriminate against any form of plant life. When I saw those dandies growing tall and strong, I was happy.

I did feel a tad uneasy when I watched them developing day after day, but the satisfaction of successful propagation overcame any suspicions I had.

Then, one day, I found myself coming face to face with reality. Someone told me that I could get arrested for growing this crop. But, I protested, it was just an experiment in horticulture ... like any other. I wasn't going to sell it, use it, or give it away.

Tough toenails, they said. It's *illegal*.

I was outraged! There were people I knew who were gasping and dying of emphysema and lung cancer from smoking ordinary tobacco. And it was legal to sell, buy, and use. Highly addictive or not. And I could be prosecuted for just *growing* those innocent little plants? But I knew I had to do something.

Sadly, I lined up my beautiful homegrown babies and looked at them for the last time. Then, I slowly dumped them all on the hard dirt floor of my plant shelter and stomped them to death. It seemed the thing to do at the time

Much has happened since those days. I now wish I could have legally donated my marijuana plants toward the relief of pain in patients with cancer, HIV, glaucoma, multiple sclerosis, or many other conditions. According to Dr. Kenneth Mayer, professor of medicine and community health at Brown University, "Marijuana, smoked, vaporized, or ingested, can indeed provide relief in some circumstances when other medicines fail." Professor Mayer goes on to say that patients who might otherwise discontinue accepted treatments for serious illnesses because of noxious side effects were "far more likely to complete their medication regimens if they used marijuana."

I am happy to see this recent compassionate piece of legislation being passed by our state lawmakers and will be hoping to see the day they also, when appropriate in extreme cases, make physician-assisted suicide legally available.

BIRDWATCHING ON
THE HIGHWAY

April 26, 2001

It was a pleasure to hear that the state Department of Transportation is giving motorists, nature lovers and summer visitors to our area a treat by installing dozens of birdhouses along Route 4 suitable for nesting tree-swallows, titmice, chickadees and especially those sometimes hard-to-find beauties, bluebirds.

Butterflies, the report says, also will be attracted to the area by the planting of wildflowers. The aim of these enterprises is to make getting stuck in heavy beach traffic more interesting. Indeed, seeing bluebirds and nodding daisies might make it down right enjoyable for the summer motorists.

Reading about the local birds brought back the flood of reminiscence about those in California. While not really a qualified birdwatcher, I have wonderful memories of the birds, the sights and sounds of them. Especially those cries of the California quail, which were always around our place in the hills, groups of them, topknots bobbing, pecking away in the brush, keeping in constant vocal contact with one another.

Neighbors down the road from us kept peacocks. In their breeding season these were resplendent with tail feathers spread and their distinctive plaintive calls that could be heard for considerable distances.

Peacocks usually stay close to home, but there was one memorable morning when we awoke to peacock voices sounding unusually loud and, looking out, we observed peacocks in an oak tree in our yard. These are very large birds, and it was a bit of a shock to realize that they could fly. The owner soon arrived with some tidbits and managed to lure them back home.

An especially unforgettable scene occurred one afternoon when I sat reading on a small patio on the hill above our house. All around were the native plants and bushes that grew there naturally and undisturbed. A rushing sound suddenly made me turn to look toward a nearby small clearing, where I saw a beautiful cock pheasant and his harem of a half-dozen or more females. I stayed very still for as long as possible while the pheasants foraged in the brush not 20 feet away until a breeze ruffled the pages of my book and the birds rose with a flourish and disappeared over the hill.

Perhaps the most interesting of the birds I saw in California was the variety I first observed when we were visiting the home of a friend when we were newcomers. From her picture window, we saw the bird moving along her driveway, long beak stretched out in front, long tail behind, churning along on powerful legs, much resembling an arrow. When it came near, it stopped and stared at us. A crest on its head popped up like a cockatoo's and its tail assumed a perky upright position. Its feathers were grayish brown, its legs and feet blue, and behind each eye was a piece of blue and orange skin.

"What is it?" I whispered.

My friend smiled. "Meet *Geococcyx californianus*," she said. "Better known as the roadrunner. The most completely western bird. You won't find him in any other part of the world."

"But ... doesn't he fly at all?"

"Not unless he has to," she said. "He always prefers to walk or run."

Doing a bit of research, I found that this big bird is 20 to 24 inches long with a strong, hooked-tip bill. *Geococcyx* means "earth cuckoo." The roadrunner is not as cuckoo as he looks but he is earthy. While other more ethereal birds are dipping and soaring through the sky, the roadrunner sticks to the ground, even building his platform nest of sticks and grasses in spiky cactus or in low branches of trees or chaparral.

Both parents take turns incubating the four or five light-colored eggs, from which emerge featherless, black-skinned babies. Once hatched, the parents are kept busy supplying their brood with their favorite food: lizards. These are killed and fed whole to the babies and the sight of the ugly nestling—with a tail hanging out of its mouth as it digests the rest of the lizard—presents a picture only a mother could love.

This bird is a real showoff, and they say he loves to race in front of mounted riders. On his long legs, he has no trouble keeping ahead of the horses.

In California, it was fun to occasionally watch a roadrunner … but, in truth, I'd rather catch a rare glimpse of Eastern bluebirds any day.

ANOTHER KIND OF FALL

October 26, 2000

Today is an October miracle of blue sky, balmy breezes, and heart-stopping blazes of autumn color ... The sort of day I dreamed about during many fall seasons in California. A time when homesickness for New England would be acute ... A time when a letter from a friend back East enclosing some scarlet and gold leaves would bring tears. But I always knew I would come back someday to live here once again.

Autumn in Southern California is not that region's finest hour. The landscape, so verdant and green in spring, has had many months without rain. The earth, the chaparral-covered hills have all dried ... often dangerously. The fall season is the time when winds blowing in from the desert can fan the smallest wisp of flame into a holocaust of fire. It happens every year in one or another of the vulnerable areas. It's expected. Until the rainy season arrives, along in early winter, there is always a threat.

Having lived half one's life on the West Coast and half on the East brings a strange and haunting dichotomy. When I was out there, I thought longingly of New England. And here, even with the season in its full glory, walking on carpets of fallen leaves beneath canopies of gorgeous color, I sometimes feel a pang of nostalgia for California ... or perhaps it's really for the life we lived there.

I especially remember taking our collie Vicky, Tyler's offspring, for strolls down the narrow dirt road from our place to a small park. Returning from one of those morning walks, I made some notes in my journal:

"It is a day of stillness and clarity. The air, for a change, is almost pure. There is just a trace of smoke left to remind us of the disasters of the past few days ... that and the blackened hills above the park. We've just experienced a horrifying succession of brush fires in these parched hills, whipped by gale-like Santana winds from the desert. At midnight, Friday, we got out of bed to help neighbors remove their valuables from their house as flames roared in the brush close by. Firemen saved the day. The, early Sunday, fires broke out again … Quite a few homes were lost and we luckier ones stood by with cars loaded with possessions awaiting the signal to evacuate which happily never came. Now, we are reasonably safe."

I go on to describe the park. *The lawns have been kept green in spite of the drought. The dog flops down and does a back-scratching dance in the cool grass. The graceful old oaks have been carefully preserved and rustic fences built around them. A covey of California quail, their top-knots bobbing, run among the ancient trees, calling to one another. A pair of red-headed woodpeckers are drumming on a blue-gum eucalyptus. A beautiful white pouter pigeon, his tail spread like a ladies fan, and a pair of greys with feathery feet peck nearby. They resemble a magnificently garbed potentate and two members of his harem.*

My eyes go to the hills. These are not the green pine-covered hills of my childhood. These are made of sandstone boulders, chunky brown rocks with accents of dark green scrub-oak and chaparral. They jut up in staggered rows, one behind the other, like stage scenery. At first, the eye accustomed to lushness finds the rocks stark and uninteresting like the surface of the moon. But given time, their charm reveals itself. You grow to appreciate their subtle tones of tan, beige, and gold against the blue sky … The pattern of the shadows they cast in late afternoon, the purity of moonlight illuminating them on a clear night.

The rocks are constant, changing imperceptibly over the years. Eons ago, they rested on the floor of the long-receded ocean. Imprints of seashells are sometimes found imbedded in them. Vicky has decided to investigate the pigeons. She approaches them slowly, with no real menace. The white pouter plants himself out in front defiantly and keeps his cool until the dog is within a few feet. Then the birds rise, wheel in formation in a graceful arc and land on a rock high on the hill.

As we reach home, Vicky lies down in the shade of an orange tree for a nap. I gaze back toward the blackened hills. Many fires have passed over them. In among the ashes, seeds of hardy plants lie waiting for the winter rains. Roots of oak and sumac with seared tops grasp the earth and gather their forces to send forth new growth.

A small white cloud comes over the horizon. Soon, very soon, the rains will come.

I am glad that I kept these records of another kind of autumn, another phase of life.

L.A. FIRE

November 13, 2003

Our house on the hill that almost burned.

R eceiving mail about the recent devastating fires across California brought back many vivid thoughts of our years there. One former neighbor, referring to the trauma in her area, says, "It got very scary in the Valley and Simi this week but the fire lines held. Ken [her cousin] had the fire burn right up to his fence!" She goes on to tell how other people on the street where we all lived were "packed and on fire watch until midnight when the wind shifted." Many homes were evacuated, however, and communication lines were jammed or burned out, making it impossible to check on friends and loved ones.

Such tales were, sad to say, not unusual over the time we were living in Southern California. Back in the early 1970s however, one event stands out. My personal account of that fire, entitled, "A Family's Life Nearly Goes Up in Smoke," appeared on the op-ed pages of The Los Angeles Times, as follows:

It's a hot afternoon in the San Fernando Valley. Cool inside, near the air conditioner. Unbearable outside.

You're sitting in the living room talking to your son. Relaxed, hanging loose. He's 27, a psychologist working in a home for disturbed children.

Your husband comes into the room from his studio, where he's been working on a speech.

"Do you smell smoke?"

You sniff the air. It's acrid, strong.

Outdoors it's even worse. Your son heads for the path that goes straight up from the house to the top of the hill. In a moment he's back, yelling, "Call the Fire Department!" He grabs a shovel and turns back toward the hill.

The smoke is billowing now. You remember the words of a neighbor: "When you see the smoke moving fast, that's it!"

Your husband is on the roof, dragging a hose, setting up a sprinkler. The big sprinklers on the hill are now spouting full force.

Sirens. They're coming.

Your heart races. Can't get your breath. You swallow a tranquilizer.

Your husband yells from the roof. "Take what you can and get out!"

What to take? The box with old family papers … letters from the sea captains and the whaler, from the Revolution and the War of 1812. They're in a dress box, top of the closet. Hands shaking, clumsy. Take the jewel box, too, the cameras. A handful of family pictures.

Down to the car. Fumbling. The jewel box slips. Down on hands and knees, grabbing at Grandma's ring, her cameo. Into the car.

A helicopter circles over the hills.

Upstairs again. The puppy follows you inside, panicked.

Your son scoops up the puppy.

The smoke is bad now. Can't see. Can't breathe.

Your husbands voice again, urgent. "Get out of the house!"

Grab the collie. Your new coat, one dress. One suit for your husband. Down to the car.

You remember the house guests, away for the day. Get their bags.

A crackling noise. Don't look towards the flames. Keep moving. Don't faint.

Fire engines block ends of the circular drive. Your son jumps into the driver's seat and guides the car around them. Then he stops, jumps out and disappears into the smoke again.

The dogs in the back seat are frightened. They trample the dress box and old letters spill out.

You can't see the house anymore. Mouth dry, nose dripping, hair falling into your eyes. You grab a neighbor's hose and wash your face.

Be steady. Stop crying. Neighbors are coming. One brings a towel, another offers tissues.

Planes overhead now, dropping water and borate.

Voices shouting. Your husband and son have disappeared behind the smoke curtain.

People are driving up ... sightseers, smiling and excited. Okay. It's not their house that's threatened. You remember the last fire you stopped to watch and you feel ashamed.

The smoke is starting to clear a little. Maybe the house won't burn.

You start up the hill.

The mop-up crew arrives. Young men with shiny metal hats.

Capable looking, efficient. They file briskly off the truck.

You can see the house clearly now. It's untouched! Your knees go weak.

A fireman is leaning against his truck, sweating, exhausted.

"You fellas did a great job," your husband says.

The fireman grins, wearily. "You were lucky. Not much wind today, thank God."

You sit down shakily, and look at the ancient, mortgaged, demanding, too small, beautiful house.

"Amen," you say.

OUT-FOXED

August 10, 2000

This year, my garden can be described as an English country garden gone wild. Two things, the extensive weather and an injury to my foot, have kept my garden cultivation to a minimum. Thank heaven for the hardy snow perennials like gloriosa daisies and lilies, which take some of the focus off rampant weeds and grasses. Wild flowers are also allowed to bloom without fear of being evicted. I find they make a good cover for toads, which are welcome, and the occasional garter snake or two ... and butterflies love them.

I was delighted to find that a small snake has a home under the front entrance to my house. Several mornings, I have found it taking the sun in a little crevice beside the front door. I can't tell how long it is because half the body remains inside its hole under the doorsill. I always say good morning, and the snake always darts out its tongue. We are sympatico.

When we lived in California, our house against the rocky hills was also a paradise for nature. There were deer, coyotes, bobcats and even the occasional mountain lion. And in the late summer and early fall, the foxes.

I'd read Aesop's fable about the fox eating the grapes but never took it seriously until one fall when fruit on our grape vines in the field below the house began to ripen. Black Ribier and amber-colored Molyneaux hanging in fragrant clusters were evidently too great a temptation for the bushy-tails. We first became aware of it when a neighbor called rather late one night.

"You'd better have a look," he said. "I think Vicky is after the foxes."

"The what?"

"Foxes," he said. "We've been hearing them barking the last few nights."

During the brief conversation, I could hear our collie's excited yelps in the distance, and as soon as I hung up I got out the flashlight and went to investigate. The dog came to meet me, out-foxed, but obviously pleased with herself for having routed the intruders.

The next night, I heard the foxes myself. They had a sharp, hoarse bark, which was quickly followed by the outraged cries of the collie. Not wanting to bother the neighbors, I rose and called in the dog, leaving the foxes to go about their business. And their business, it turned out, was eating grapes. Not that we minded. There was more than enough fruit for everybody, including the birds and the foxes. If they'd only be quiet about it.

Several nights later, when it all began again, I called in Vicky, who came inside reluctantly, and flashlight in hand, I made my way in the direction of the sounds. I arrived at the edge of a small meadow and stood waiting in the shadow of an olive tree. At first nothing moved. And then the black cat, Dolores, who had followed me, pricked up her ears, turned abruptly and ran back toward the house.

I turned off the flashlight and waited. The first fox appeared suddenly. He was gray and small, only a little larger than a full-grown house cat. His ears were longer than a cat's and so were his legs, and his tail was magnificently bushy. He was soon joined by another, perhaps his mate. I stood very still.

It was a night of brilliant moonlight. The stars appeared very close … as though hung on strings from the ceiling of the sky. The foxes, I felt, couldn't help knowing that I was there but they ignored me and began to play.

They frolicked, they gamboled, and yes, they seemed to dance. With little mincing steps they would advance, then jump in the air and run out of sight only to appear again suddenly and chase one another in little circles like dogs at play. They must have just dined royally on prime table grapes and were celebrating … celebrating the night and each other. And I was allowed to be a spectator. I felt very privileged.

It was all over in a few minutes. With a final flirt of their handsome tails, they disappeared over the hill and I went back to my bed.

"Ah, well," I thought, as I settled back. "For a sight such as that I don't mind missing some sleep."

And that was no sour grapes!

AN OLD RANCHER AND
THE MANSON FAMILY

July 30, 2000

Before mail-in census forms, there were census takers who went door to door, asking questions about marriage, family, children and ethnicity. Thirty years ago, in southern California, I was one of them. Just before the end of my final training period, in 1970, our instructor gave out assignments.

We were to cover territories nearest our homes, and I drew the Twin Lakes section of Chatsworth. In those days, it was a place of Indian trails, boulders, rotten roads, and individuals whose names in the register bore annotations such as "He carries a gun," "Don't approach suddenly" and "Very fierce dog."

Almost as an afterthought, our instructor told me, "By the way, you also have to cover the Spahn Ranch."

People gasped. The 1969 murders of actress Sharon Tate and six others by Charles Manson and his devotees were still fresh in our minds. The plot had been hatched at the Spahn Movie Ranch, where the near-blind 81-year-old owner, George Spahn, had been conned into allowing "the family" to live.

Manson and five others were in custody, awaiting trial, but many of his followers were still living at the ranch. I had seen them in town on their "garbage runs"; disheveled and glowering, they would collect discarded fruits and vegetables from behind markets. Although their guru was detained, they believed it was only a matter of time before he would be back with them.

"Of course," the census instructor continued, "you don't have to get the names of all those hippies up there. Just the permanent ones. And you can take a policeman along."

"Fat chance!" I said to myself. As a writer, here was my opportunity to venture into the Manson stronghold and maybe dredge up an angle that hadn't been covered by the hordes of journalists. I had no intention of taking the fuzz along.

In addition, George Spahn was a neighbor of sorts. The now-run-down ranch, where cowboys and Indians had once galloped in B-grade movies, was just a few rock-strewn, chaparral-covered hills behind our place, across the Southern Pacific railroad tracks. Before the Manson people arrived, in the late '60s, we'd seen the old man riding around town in his old truck with "Spahn's Movie Ranch" on the side, driven by his ranch manager and sidekick, Ruby Pearl, a former bare-back rider.

But after the Manson Family moved in, we didn't see much of Spahn. According to rumor, the young women kept him occupied with food and sex to the point that he never knew nor cared what was going on in his home. Ruby Pearl was still on the scene, but her responsibilities as manager ended at dusk, when she went home. The only other member of the Spahn household was the ranch hand, Donald "Shorty" Shea, but he had disappeared soon after the murders. It was thought that the part-time movie cowboy had gone after an acting job, as he had done in the past.

I had spoken to Spahn only once during the decade since we moved to Chatsworth. Our young sons and their pals loved to roam the hills, where deer, foxes, bobcats, and the occasional mountain lion lived. We were glad the boys were enjoying nature and tried not to worry too much about rattlesnakes and the like. But one thing out there worried me – the kids had discovered an uncovered well – or was it a mine shaft? They reported that anyone could've stumbled and fallen in. It was so deep, they said, that when they dropped rocks into it, they never heard them hit the bottom. From their description, it seemed the shaft was located on the Spahn Ranch, and I called Spahn to complain. He promised to take care of it, but as long as we lived there, I don't believe he did.

It was a hot day in April when I turned off the old Santa Susana Pass Road and drove the couple of miles to the Spahn property. There, under the broiling sun, a sagging "Movie Ranch" sign led into a dusty yard and a cluster of ancient buildings still sporting names such as Longhorn

Saloon and Rock City Café. Two filthy horse wranglers eyed me as I stepped out briskly, juggling a 3-pound census satchel, and a clipboard and pen.

"Where can I find Mr. Spahn?" I asked.

One of them pointed toward a building. I knocked on the door, and after a considerable delay, it was opened by a rather scruffy woman in a ragged skirt and a man's shirt. I introduced myself and asked to see Mr. Spahn. She eyed me coldly for a moment and then stepped back, leaving the door ajar. I walked in.

The room was so dark that I couldn't see a thing at first. My other senses more than made up for the deficiency, however. There were smells—indescribable cooking smells, animal smells, dust. And there was a loud buzzing; flies everywhere.

I eventually made out a round table in one corner that held the remains of a meal; amid the mess, two large cats sat scrounging tidbits. Along one wall was an old sofa on which a large saddle rested. And at the far end of the room, I could detect a stove and sink, both black with age and grime.

As my eyes adjusted to the light, I saw two young women, who appeared to be cooking and eyeing me suspiciously. I could now distinguish the seated figure of George Spahn, sporting his cowboy hat and dark glasses, talking on the phone. The octogenarian, I noticed, was still quite a handsome man.

The woman who had answered the door approached me, hands on hips. She was small, skinny and freckled, with red hair. She looked vaguely familiar. Had I seen her in town? (I later realized that this was probably Lynette "Squeaky" Fromme, who had been assigned by Manson to take care of Spahn, to be his eyes, his assistant, his bedfellow, and to report on all his conversations and ensure that no one got close enough to spoil the family's setup at the ranch.)

The woman stared at me. "Whaddya want?" she asked.

I stated my business and she laughed derisively. The two girls who were cooking joined in. "You want my name?" the redhead said. "I'm Greta Garbo. And that's Marilyn Monroe," she said, pointing.

The door opened, and the two surly cowboys came in. "She's from the census," the skinny woman told them, and then said to me: "This here's Humphrey Bogart."

I was happy to remember my instructions: "You don't have to get names of all those hippies up there. Just the permanent ones."

"Mr. Spahn," I said, "I'm here to help you fill out your census form. I'll try to make it as brief as possible."

Spahn smiled and nodded and I proceeded to ask him all the questions about himself and his living quarters. He answered willingly enough. The red-haired woman moved closer to him, fixing me with a cold stare.

While this was going on, more women and men entered the house. It was getting a bit crowded, not to mention fetid. I finished the questions about Spahn and his house and, having decided to narrow the "permanent residents" down to one, I asked about the ranch hand.

Spahn didn't answer right away. The room was suddenly very still, except for the buzzing of flies. I thought maybe he hadn't heard me.

"You have a ranch hand who lives here, don't you, Mr. Spahn? Is his name Shea?"

Something caused me to look up. The eyes of perhaps 10 people were all focused on me.

I had a sudden flash of what I represented to these people. Not the war-protesting, civil-rights-advocating liberal I believed myself to be, but a personification of the Enemy. I was someone of the generation from which they had cut all ties, a member of the Establishment and a person conducting a government survey who might just be a police spy. I thought of the Manson Family's epithet, PIG, written in blood at one of the murder sites, and I regretted my decision not to take a police officer.

After what seemed like a very long pause, Spahn answered, simply, that Shea wasn't there anymore. I hastily got Spahn's signature and, with trembling hands, put my materials in my satchel and turned to go.

I passed through the room and, to my immense relief, was allowed to walk out by those standing nearest the door. Outside, I could still feel their eyes on me, and I said a prayer for my car to start.

Back home, still shaking, I reviewed what had just happened. Had I imagined the danger?

By Manson's later admission and the testimony of other family members, the ranch hand, Shorty Shea, had tried to warn George Spahn about them, and so was stabbed and hacked to death. (Shea's remains were found in a shallow grave adjacent to the ranch.) Squeaky Fromme, of course, became infamous a few years later for attempting to take a shot at President Ford. And in his book, "Helter Skelter," the prosecutor in the Manson case, Vincent Bugliosi, quotes a Manson follower as saying that the family killed a total of 35 to 40 people, some of them after the Tate-LaBianca murders.

In late September of 1970, the Spahn Ranch and much of Chatsworth burned in a brush fire. The ranch land was then sold to a developer. But I wonder if anyone ever looked down that deep well, where kids used to drop rocks and never heard them hit the bottom.

PART SIX

BETWEEN COURSES

Gerry Leaper, a first generation American with roots from Galway, Ireland, shown here in a photograph from his acting portfolio.

VISITING GALWAY

April 23, 1998

If you ever travel o'er the sea to Ireland,
Then maybe at the closing of the day,
You will see the moonlight rising over Claddagh,
and watch the sun go down on Galway Bay.

—Irish Song

"So you want to trace your relations?" O'Halloran the cobbler spoke from the side of his mouth, the while holding a couple of nails between his teeth. We had just stopped in at his shop in Galway, Ireland, to inquire if he could put new heels on my old comfortable walking shoes.

Having been assured that he could, we had started to depart, planning to return later with the shoes.

"Leave them," he stated emphatically.

"But, I've none with me to wear," I protested.

"Sit down, Missus. I'll have them for you in a jiffy."

So now I sat in my stocking feet, my husband leaning on the counter, as we watched O'Halloran deftly carve two round circles from a piece of leather, pound in nails and trim the excess from the heels, at the same time keeping up a conversation, his ruddy face aglow with amiability and, no doubt, a drop of "Irish cheer."

Having learned that my husband's parents came from Galway and we were interested in finding kinfolk, he laughed.

"Sure and it just came over the radio," he said, indicating a small set on his bench, "in County Mayo, they're drivin' the church clerks crazy. Three bus-loads of Americans drove up at once … all tryin' to dig up their ancestors. Most of 'em have to look back four or five generations and a fire in 1860 destroyed all the records. The poor fellas are goin' daft."

173

Our meeting with O'Halloran took place a couple of decades ago. We had gone to Eire with the long-cherished desire to see the places and people we heard so much about, especially from my husband's mother, a woman of charm with a great talent for story-telling.

After a week in Dublin, we drove across the country to Galway, where we rented a flat and settled in for three months of painting and writing and soaking up the environment.

Trying to keep warm also occupied a good deal of time since we got there in early October and stayed until Christmas in a house, like most Irish houses, without central heating. The warmth of the people made up for it, however.

Gerry, newly retired as a staff member of a university, had only family last names to go by, but in a small city like Galway, that was enough. Before long, he located the address of a cousin, the daughter of his mother's brother. Sine there was no phone listed, one day he went directly to her house and rang the bell.

This good lady opened the door and saw a complete stranger who announced, "I think I'm your cousin," and gave a brief explanation.

May Fahey opened her arms and embraced him. "Glory be to God," she said. "Sure and you've got my father's eyes!"

Soon, we were both invited to her house to meet her family and have tea. Hearing about Gerry's fondness for his mother's Irish soda bread, she baked some, and even made him Irish potato cakes, a laborious process that I never could master.

May and her daughter accompanied us on a drive into the wild, tree-less moonscape of Connemara and into the village where much of the John Wayne movie, "The Quiet Man," was filmed.

We met all kinds of people in Galway—artists, fishermen, monks, merchants and the "tinkers," or Irish gypsies, usually referred to as "itinerants." We found the building in town where Gerry's grandmother, the mother of 12 children, once ran a small grocery store, meeting the needs of local farmers and townspeople. We visited the churches, the castle ruins and the green countryside where Gerry's parents had grown up and courted and from where his father left Trinity College in Dublin and later won a scholarship to Oxford University.

We saw Yeats's Tower, where the poet wrote his works and Coole

Park, the former estate of Lady Gregory. As the Irish say, it was a lovely time.

The current news of the expected success of a peace pact that may eventually bring to an end the terrible conflicts that both Northern Irish and the people of the Republic have suffered for years is indeed wonderful.

Long may they endure and prosper.

A HOLIDAY IN ERIN

November 20, 1998

Thanksgiving Day
A time to share,
A time to say
A grateful prayer.

This year, Thanksgiving Day falls on the same November date as the first official national Thanksgiving proclaimed by George Washington on Nov. 26, 1789. Since the original holiday observed by the Plymouth Colony in 1621, when Pilgrims, grateful for a bountiful harvest after a winter of starvation and great suffering, sat down with some of the local Native Americans to enjoy a feast, similar celebrations were held only sporadically until Washington's time. It took a joint resolution of Congress in 1941, however, to decree that Thanksgiving should occur on the fourth Thursday in November.

Can you imagine what it must have been like to be a member of that small group of colonists? To really get into the proper frame of mind, you would have to take a walk into the woods ... out of sight and sound of human habitation, and imagine being without food, medical aid, proper shelter or hope of help for a long period of time. To exist in a strange and harsh land during endless snow-filled winters depending entirely on what you and the other colonists could grow or hunt for with a primitive musket. To be always at the mercy of the elements or sometimes unfriendly Indians.

No wonder those first settlers felt they must give thanks for a plentiful harvest and had a desire to share it with Chief Massasoit and his band of men who joined them in the spirit of good will. And who, according to legend, did not come empty-handed but brought deer meat and corn to the feast.

As time goes by, it seems increasingly important to me that we keep traditions alive, and Thanksgiving is certainly the holiday most closely associated with New England. Its spirit, however, can be celebrated wherever you happen to be.

When my husband and I were staying in Ireland for some time, the November date was approaching, and we decided not to let it pass unnoticed. We were renting the upper floor of a private house. The landlady and her daughter, a nurse, lived on the first floor. Like most Irish houses, this one had no central heat. Each of our four rooms had its individual coin-operated heating unit. Downstairs, the seldom-used parlor, was an artic zone. The owners stayed in their warm shut-off kitchen area, which had a peat fire going most of the time.

Most of our activity in the house centered on a sort of family room, a former bedroom now equipped with a small stove, refrigerator, table and chairs, and a sofa. We could put coins in the heater, have a meal, and watch our rented TV set, and stay warm until bedtime. This was where we decided to hold our Thanksgiving dinner.

Galway, a small city on the west coast of Ireland, has a lot in common with New England coastal towns. It faces the open Atlantic, often stormy and unpredictable. Also, like those coastal towns, it has been home to generations of fishermen. In addition, it is a bustling center of activity of various kinds but still retains a distinctive character. Shopping for a turkey, we knew, would be useless, so we bought two fat roasting chickens. From the farmers' market, we got vegetables and some currant jelly in place of cranberry sauce. And for dessert, steamed plum pudding and minced tarts.

We invited our landlady, Mary, and her daughter, Rita, as well as a young American couple we met while food shopping, to share our feast. With a bit of wine and good conversation, we all enjoyed our Irish Thanksgiving that year.

A family of Irish "Tinkers," sometimes called "Itinerants," pictured in 1977

BRING BACK GLORY DAYS OF RAIL

December 28, 2001

I have to admit to being a train enthusiast, one who refuses to succumb to the current depressing mind-set about the future of rail travel in this country. I will continue to keep positive thoughts about it no matter how many dire predictions and reports of failure are expressed. I have to admit, though, a lot has to be done to make train service available, serviceable and affordable to the general public. It should be as it once was, an interesting and enjoyable experience.

The government-sponsored rail program, Amtrak, has been in bad financial straits for some time now, but signs of hope are forthcoming from legislative proposals. Many believe that traveling by train should continue to be an essential, available choice for Americans. Many thorny problems must be solved, though.

A close family member, a young woman traveling with her five-month-old infant, told me today of her recent "train trip from hell" going from San Francisco to St. Louis. The trip took four days, including having to travel a long distance by bus because of some connection mistake, and ended with half her luggage being left behind in California.

Unfortunately, such stories are not all that rare. A few months ago, cherishing fond memories of former train trips across the country, I visited a local station to inquire about taking a trip to California. I listened incredulously as the man behind the ticket window pointed out that such a journey involved four days, three nights, changing trains in Chicago, and including the minimum sleeping accommodation, would cost in the neighborhood of $1,700! How could that be, I inquired, since the trip formerly only took three days and two nights and was a whole lot cheaper? He shrugged and leaning forward, confided, "I could go free," he said, "but I'd fly anyway."

No wonder business is bad!

Another person told me glowingly about her recent trip from Washington to Rhode Island on the Acela ... the fast electric train. "It just skims along," she trilled, "you don't hear or feel anything."

"But can you enjoy the sights, the scenery, going that fast?" I asked.

"No, you don't see anything, either," she said.

Traveling at 100 mph with the world a blur outside is not my idea of a train trip. Especially when I recall the Super Chief and other pre-Amtrak journeys so fondly. It's true they took place several decades ago, but they still remain in the treasure-trove of memory, waiting to be refreshed by looking through my diary notes, such as those made during a cross-country trip from California to New England.

Sept. 24

Saw the sun rise over Northern Arizona this morning. From the window of my roomette, I watched the color change from gold to rose to violet. The scene also changed from flat grazing lands to pines as we approached Williams south of the Grand Canyon.

Here the elevation is more than 6,000 feet and tall pines are abundant.

... This afternoon I spend several hours in the dome-liner, where the view spreads out for miles. Passed through some beautiful country of Northern New Mexico. Red hills, blue asters and some other yellow wildflowers ... rocks, trees ... many native adobe Indian and Mexican dwellings ... some cattle and sheep.

Have had conversations with some other travelers ... three ladies on their way to New England and Canada to see the fall foliage. Got off at Albuquerque when the train made a 20-minute stop. We are approaching the New Mexico-Colorado boundary. There are many clouds in the sky and a rainbow. It must be raining up ahead ... Now it is flat farm and grazing land with buttes sticking up here and there ... Had a marvelous chat with a young man from Ireland on his way back to Europe. Talked for two hours.

Sept. 25

We pulled into Kansas City about 5:30 a.m. Beginning to see pretty country, rivers, trees, green meadows. Couldn't get enough of looking at the landscape. William, the Irishman, gave me his parents' address in Dublin in case I ever got over there. Also have made a friend ... a black woman from Los Angeles who had the roomette next to mine. Her name is Gladys and we have the same kind of sense of humor. Laughed all the way to Chicago, especially when we had lunch with a woman from Texas, a dead-ringer for actor Chill Wills.

Sept. 26

Gladys and I arrived in New York, raced across Grand Central Station and got on the train for New England. She got off at New Haven, Connecticut, while I continued on to Providence.

I missed her as soon as she was gone, but sadly, we never met again.

Traveling by train used to be a real trip and an enriching experience. Let's hope that one day soon it will become that way again.

PART SEVEN

SECOND HELPINGS

GOING BACK FOR MORE

I've always wondered who Thomas Wolfe had in mind when he said, "you can't go home again." Certainly not me, a woman who left Rhode Island for California, putting her family semi-heirlooms into a moving company's warehouse and keeping them there for three decades!

Aunt Min's grand piano, great-grandmother's dining room table, grandma's cut glass, the 200-year-old milking stool, and all the rest of what irreverent male relatives refer to as "that old stuff." My insurance, you might say, an "I shall return" promise to all those Yankee ancestors.

In California, we ended up in the San Fernando Valley to "make it our home," as the song said. Only Mom had a plan. "Don't sink roots down too far in the adobe soil. "Someday, we'll go back to New England," I told them.

Nobody really believed it. "Sure, Ma, sure," the boys said, growing up California-style. We did the whole bit. Lived first in Hollywood, then in the Valley. Took trips to the redwoods, the desert, the Pacific. Did quite a lot of acting in theater, in television and lots of years working in the aerospace industry for Dad and writing for me. And then, suddenly, it's retirement time.

The boys were long since grown, one of the granddaughters just starting college. The house, with the two acres of rocks, oleanders, eucalyptus, California poppies, and gophers, was sold and our plan began to take shape.

You've got to be kidding! How could you take that climate back there?" a friend said, standing outside the market in 100-degree temperature, peering through the murky yellow of a first-stage smog alert.

"Nobody goes back." My doctor stared at me incredulously and made a remark about examining my head.

"I do," I said. "It's home. It's always been home."

My husband looked a bit grim but he was game. An easterner himself, he was willing to give it a try. Our sons, their lives built around jobs and homes in California, bid us a wistful but still skeptical farewell.

HOME AGAIN

We left Los Angeles on June 7, 1984. Not an auspicious day, as it turned out. Stepping off the plane in Boston, we walked out of Logan Airport into a Turkish bath. Temperature 96 degrees. Humidity roughly the same ... And it stayed that way for days. A week later, we got caught in probably the worst electrical storm of the century.

"Well, how do you like it so far?" my husband said.

"It'll get better," I said through clenched teeth.

And, of course, it did. True to tradition, the weather changed. It got cooler, the humidity dropped, the countryside was gorgeous. Gerry began to take on the look of a convert. It was the air that got to him. Ocean-scented, pine-scented, no smog-scented air.

And so we ended up buying a home ... an old house in a tiny village close by an historic gristmill. The house needed paint, a new roof, a new septic tank, and plenty of cosmetic work inside. But there were lilacs by the back door, two fireplaces, a flowing stream with a waterfall nearby and a small barn to make into a painting studio for Gerry. When we had moved in, we brought the "old stuff" out of storage and found that despite signs of age and wear and tear, they fitted into our old house like the missing pieces of a puzzle.

The hardest part, of course, was leaving our family back on the West Coast. One son has come here and re-settled not too far away. The other has visited with his wife and daughters, and after sniffing the ocean air, looking down from the Jamestown Bridge at the deep blue bay, walking the beautiful sandy beaches and dropping a line into lovely little trout ponds, understands a little better the homesickness that never left me during all those years in California.

Now, as I write these words, my South County garden is ready to burst into bloom, the woods behind the house are filled with singing birds, and all seems right with the world.

A local cynic might say, "What about next February? Remember the winter of '78?"

All I can say is, "Seems like that's about the time to visit the kids in California for a couple of weeks."

I may be sentimental, but I'm not stupid.

MEMORIES OF SUMMER
STORMS PAST

August 24, 2000

In the midst of a summer that has featured more than the usual cold, rainy days, today brings New England weather at its most memorable. Beautifully sunny, yet cool with just enough of a light breeze in the garden to gently sway the nodding flowers. A day that makes you wish it could be cloned and kept forever. Still, we have the autumn to look forward to … and for me, that is the best season.

The welcome rains of this summer have had their price. Quite a few gloomy, cloudy days that can dampen the spirits of people and pets. Being shut up in the house on a cloudy, rainy day with two cats, I've found, can be similar to being confined with two young children. In fact, worse in some ways. Kids old enough to go out and play can understand that you are not responsible for the inclement weather, whereas felines take your seemingly contrary refusal to bring forth sunshine as a personal affront. They stand accusingly by the door and stare at you with that look that says, "If you wanted to, you could change it." Cats are experts at generating guilt.

With the fall approaching fast there are already reports coming daily about hurricanes forming. At this point, they are far away down in the distant Atlantic; not even a threat to the Caribbean islands. Most of us, however, know that it's a good bet that one or more will eventually make its way north and maybe even touch our shores. In our perennial optimism, we give the possibility little attention and keep right on building houses, condos and other dwellings perilously close to the sea. A fatalistic attitude tends to prevail, just as it does on the earthquake-imperiled West Coast and the whole Western U.S. fire-threatened area. Homes without a chance in Hades of withstanding nature's upheavals are regularly erected in vulnerable spots. Makes you speculate about our so-called superior intelligence.

Half of my life has been lived in Southern California and half in New England, so there have been ample opportunities to see what can happen. A scary scenario took place when my husband, two young sons, and I first moved to Los Angeles and had a house in Hollywood Hills. We were awakened at 2:30 one morning by a violent shaking that nearly knocked us out of our beds. Trying to make our way into the children's room resulted in stumbling and falls but no real damage was done to us. There were casualties in other places, however, especially where houses had been built almost on the very edge of cliffs.

There were scares in the years that followed, but the time I remember being most fearful of quakes was lying on the sand at Santa Barbara and feeling the beach beneath me shaking. I sat up quickly and watched to see if the ocean was receding. I knew that a drastic withdrawing of water out to sea was a precursor of a tsunami—a tidal wave—that could be the result of an earthquake thousands of miles away. Luckily, no such disaster occurred, but it would be possible.

Here in Rhode Island, I've written about my experience in The Big One, the 1938 hurricane. Ironically, after spending more than 30 years in California, we came back here to live just in time for Hurricane Gloria in 1985, which happened the day before my scheduled high school reunion. Since I keep a daily journal, I've been able to turn back to that year and see what I wrote beginning Wednesday, Sept. 25, 1985.

"There's a big hurricane down in the south Atlantic which may be coming our way. Everyone is buying supplies and battening down the hatches. Our reunion may be in jeopardy."

Thursday, Sept. 26: "Hurricane on the way. They say it's headed directly for New England. Everybody's buying candles, food, batteries, etc. Gerry boarded up the kitchen windows. Put our cars away. I got more food and cooked a ham. Worried about the reunion. TV on all day to get weather reports and path of storm. We drew lots of drinking water and filled two bath tubs as well."

Friday, Sept. 27: "We got the hurricane today. Bad! But it could have been worse. First part of the day wasn't very scary but predictions were. Winds began rising about 10 a.m. Worst part was in mid-afternoon. Very little rain but lots of wind. Finally, one 100-mile-an-hour gust broke off the big pine tree south of my garden and it fell onto the kitchen roof, broke dining-room window and the back door. Gerry was trying to make a cup of tea in the kitchen when the tree trunk came through the wall. Narrowly missed him. Our power gone. Telephone still works."

Although we didn't get back the electricity for almost a week, we were lucky not to have had more serious damage.

The reunion took place as scheduled.

MAKING MUSIC

May 25, 1998

Aunt Min's piano.

B attle-scarred, but staunch, the old Gabler grand piano stood, its massive legs planted firmly on the floor of the dining room niche in the old colonial house my husband and I bought when we came back to Rhode Island a few years ago.

The piano's top lay upraised in two pieces waiting to be mended and a piece of tape holding a sizable hunk of veneer in place, but its innards had been tuned and renovated and, while its music might not meet the standards of Horowitz, to me it sounded mellow and sweet.

And did especially when my granddaughter, Laura, then a youngster, came from California to visit and sat down to play. It was then I knew why I had hung on to it and all the other stuff, paying for storage all those years. Call it tradition, call it sentiment, call it crazy. I knew I would do it all over again.

We went to live in California when our boys were small and stayed for three decades. Before we left Rhode Island, I put the things I valued, my mother's desk, the sea chest, my grandmother's china, the old love seat, and, of course, the piano, into storage.

I never brought them to the West for a variety of reasons … the cost, the fact that we never really had space for anything the size of a piano, and, secretly, because I always knew I would be returning to New England someday. The call of the place, of all those old Yankee ancestors, was too strong to keep me forever in California. And so we came back, bought an old house, fixed it up some, planted a garden, and at long last, took the stuff out of storage.

The piano was not a very pretty sight. For more than thirty years the body of it had been standing legless on its side in a cold warehouse. Its bench was missing (replaced, finally, by the storage company), but put together and tuned, it began to resemble the instrument that first my mother and then myself had learned to play on as children, both of us taught by the same teacher, my Great-Aunt Min.

Aunt Min and Aunt Nell were my grandmother's sisters, unmarried ladies who lived in what was for me a fascinating house. Aunt Min gave piano lessons and Aunt Nell was principal of a small elementary school. As an eight-year-old, on Fridays after school, I would ride the streetcar to the aunts' house, take my piano lesson, and stay overnight.

It seemed to me, in those pre-television days, that there were endless things to see and do. The aunts' house had a basement and an attic, both full of wondrous stuff. Their yard had a grape arbor, pear and apple trees, and flowers. Their library was stocked with books that, thanks to Aunt Nell's training, I could read and enjoy. In the evening, after supper, they would often read aloud, taking turns. Or we listened to the radio, played records on the Victrola, or played Parcheesi or checkers. When my dad came to pick my up in Saturday afternoon, I left with regret but with the knowledge that I could come back next week.

When the aunts were both gone, my mother inherited the piano. My mother was small and red-haired and played a mean ragtime piano. She also wrote songs and had several published before I was born. Whenever friends or relatives got together, everybody wanted to hear my mother play and sing her own songs. Then we'd all gather around the piano and sing old favorites. Often, someone would bring along a fiddle or a banjo and join in.

So it was that these many years later, when Laura sat down to play her pieces, in a kind of great sing-along memory, I could see them all standing around the piano; long-gone parents, grandparents, aunts, uncles and cousins. I felt a sense of continuity or time simultaneously stretching back into the past and forward into the future.

By the time Laura gets to be my age, the old piano probably won't be around. No matter. There will still be music; there will be memories. And the beat goes on.

YARD SALE ADVICE

May 26, 2005

Well, it's that time of year again. The weather's warming up and lots of folks feel the urge to get out and drive around looking for treasures and junk that they don't need but can't resist buying. In other words, it's Yard Sale Time!

Because we at one time conducted such an event, jointly with friends who lived around the corner, perhaps I can pass along a few suggestions.

We learned the hard way: A yard sale can be an exercise in humiliation. To minimize the sting, pick partners whose stuff is no better than yours. Our salemates were military people who had lived all over the globe and offered such things as hand-blown Mexican glass, brass vases, teak-wood cabinets, and even a harem lamp from the Middle East. In contrast, our modest (I hate to say pitiful) merchandise included items like a child's desk painted pink, a bedspread, a pair of wooden lamps, pots and pans, eclectic costume jewelry, and odds and ends.

After the time-consuming and sensitive steps of selecting and pricing articles for sale (family arguments may arise during this phase), sale day finally arrives.

We agreed to hold the sale at our place because we have the best location. Our partners drive up and unload their goods. Right away, we start exchanging white elephants. I want her terracotta strawberry jar. She has eyes for my Hire's Root Beer sign, a collectors item and probably our only valuable offering. We make a deal. (Suggestion: Don't get carried away.)

The advertised opening hour was 9 a.m. At 8, several people show up and are turned away because we aren't even set up yet. By 8:30, there are cars parked in front. Sharp-eyed "pickers," yard-sale specialists who make a business of finding good buys from resale, are lined up impatiently waiting for the word. At 8:45, we open up.

Right away, I sell the little pink desk. I had paid $8 for it at a yard sale five years ago and, exhibiting tremendous business acumen, sold it for the same price! (Suggestion: Don't be too eager.)

The morning passes. People mill around. The sun gets hot. A few items are sold, nothing over $3. I make coffee and go buy muffins for the staff. Friendly neighbors drop by to chat and offer moral support. We get the lookie-loos; we get the cranks. It's fun for some to stop and paw over your treasures and say things like, "Look, Harry, this is just like the one we tried to give the Salvation Army last week … and they wouldn't take it, ha, ha." (Suggestion: Don't lose your cool.)

I try to look nonchalant, sitting on a folding chair, pretending to read a book while watching the people out of the corner of my eye. I go in and make more coffee and cook hot dogs for the crew. There's still a lot unsold. We start lowering prices. A little girl is enthralled with the blue and yellow child's thermos, but Mommy hesitates. I hand it to the tot for 50 cents, wondering what I'm doing here and why. At 3 o'clock, we decide to pack it in. The friends load their leftovers into the van, drive a few miles and sell them to a dealer. We put our stuff back in the basement, which somehow looks even fuller than before. Later, we all meet at a local fast-food place.

Collapsing, exhausted, we look over the figures. It seems that after the cost of the newspaper ad, the poster board for signs, the snacks, the lunch and the supper, we almost broke even. But hey, it was a lovely day, we met some nice people, unloaded a few clunkers—and tomorrow I can go out and plant nasturtiums and pansies in my brand new terra-cotta strawberry jar. (Suggestion: Have a Nice Day.)

BYE BYE BIRDIE

May 13, 1999

Today, I am a home-wrecker. I have destroyed what was to have been the haven for a family ... a family of robins, that is and while I feel regret, I'm not a bit sorry.

In the room where I work, where I more or less tied to a computer, are two windows that overlook my garden on one side, and on the other, two large trees, one a maple and the other an apple tree. As with most people who write the urge to stretch one's legs, or goof off, comes often. During these intervals, I usually go over and see what's happening outside.

A good deal of the time, nothing is going on. Unless, of course, you count the changing seasons, the trees beginning to bud or leaf out, or in the autumn, turn to glorious color. Or flowers starting to bloom in the garden. In the spring, too, there are birds going about their business of nest-building. And that's what I saw when I looked out my window today. A pair of robins building a nest in the apple tree. Sounds nice. Fun to watch ... to anticipate the eggs being incubated, the nestlings hatched. All taking place right below my window. The problem is ... I was not the only one watching.

Now, birds are marvelous creatures. Beautiful, graceful, free ... but dumb. They rely almost entirely on instinct which serves them well. But the pejorative term, "bird-brain," pretty much hits the target when describing miniscule intelligence. Thus, the robins were busily building their nest in full view and easy reach of my two cats, who were overseeing the procedure with interest.

A whole tragic scenario of what might soon happen flashed across my mind and I did what I felt was unavoidable. I went outside, got a long pole, and knocked down the half-finished nest right under the noses (or beaks) of the unfortunate pair. Muttering that old disclaimer,

"It's for your own good," I'm afraid gave them, or me, little comfort. I felt terrible.

The cats were appalled. Clearly, their opinion of my actions, never very high, took a downward turn. "Spoil sport!" their eyes accused. They stalked off, lashing their tails.

With the pressure of deadlines, I knew I must get back to my desk. But under the emotional trauma of the recent incident, I had no recourse but to go to the kitchen, make a cup of tea, and have a snack. The universal stress remedy for all at-home workers.

Fortified by two cups of tea and a brownie, my burden of guilt somewhat assuaged, I finally got back to work at the computer. However, after an hour or so, the urge to stretch my legs found me once again getting up from the chair and strolling over to the window. This time, the one overlooking the garden.

What I saw now was not pleasant. A young woodchuck was in the flower garden devouring my shasta daisy plants! The ones I'd been coaxing along for the past three years and which had begun to look promising.

I flew down the stairs and out the back door to the garden area to chase away the intruder. Easier said than done, I found. A woodchuck, a.k.a. groundhog, is a fat, bristle-haired member of the rodent family, a veritable chewing machine. Its heavy body and very short legs, however, mean it is not designed for making a fast getaway. When I approached it, making shoo-ing noises, it just stood there looking at me defiantly, long leaves of shasta daisy protruding from its mouth. As I got closer, it reared up on its hind legs like a prairie dog. I picked up a piece of firewood from the nearby pile and made threatening gestures. The woodchuck dropped once again to all fours, shot me an "I shall return" look and scuttled away into the shrubbery.

Later, as I stood in line at the hardware store to buy fencing, I thought of the poet Longfellow's words, "No tears dim the sweet look that Nature gives."

It's obvious that he never came face to face with a beady-eyed, flower-chompin' woodchuck.

HOW BRAINY ARE THESE BIRDS?

June 24, 1999

Their flight is high and free,
It's true.
but do they have
a high IQ?

Following a recent column, in which I related my attempts to save a family of robins by destroying a nest being built in a vulnerable spot, I received a letter giving me a sharp rap on the knuckles for saying that birds are dumb. The writer blamed what was called my "19th-century attitudes toward the natural world." Hey, I may have been around awhile … but not that long!

The very literate and informative epistle went on to explain that birds are not stupid, they just haven't had time to develop natural defenses against predators such as domestic cats, which were introduced into the environment by the Europeans centuries ago. (My comment: They may not be dumb, but they sure are slow learners.)

The writer is obviously very bird-wise. I, admittedly, am not. I am only an admirer, an ardent observer filled with joy and awe at their beauty and a touch of envy for the ease and freedom of their flight. I'm also a person who faithfully puts out seed and suet for them all winter and nectar for hummers in summer.

The reader writes that she has "two small domestic-bred South American parrots" and says that when an image of a jaguar appears on TV, the birds will freeze and watch that picture until the image is gone and they feel safe. They do not, the letter states, react the same way to cats from other continents … not even a leopard! Now, that is smart.

There's no mention of whether these parrots can talk, but it would seem that any bird brainy enough to tell the geographic origin of a feline seen on television should be able to converse, probably in two languages. Such as...

"Buenos dias, Pedro. ¿Qué tal?"

"Not so good, Juan. Can't get any sleep."

"¿Por qué?"

"It's those darn jungle shows on TV. Did you see the size of that jaguar?"

"Si, si. ¡Uno gato malo! Maybe we should cancel that plan to fly down to Rio for the carnival."

My personal experience with talking birds is not great. I do, however, have a vivid recollection of meeting up with a mynah bird in a small and not very well-kept zoo in California. The mynah, or Asiatic starling, is a black bird about the size of a crow and is said to be a better mimic than a parrot. This one had perfect diction. Unfortunately, this individual's vocabulary appeared to be limited to two two-word phrases. Any friendly remark addressed to him, such as "Hello" or "What's your name?" was met with either one of these two responses. The printable one was "Drop dead!"

A bird with a more civil tongue in his head was a parrot owned by a couple we met while doing some theater work in California. Two sons of the family were, at the time, playing prominent roles in the television series "Little House on the Prairie." The older boy worked in a stage production of "Father of the Bride" with my husband. When we attended a party at their house we were surprised to see the parrot flying freely about the room, now and then letting out a startling cry and shouting, "Fire, fire—save the bird!" Parrot owners just can't seem to restrain their sense of whimsy.

The letter I received also said, "I ask you that you consider converting your cats to house dwellers and provide them with a safe, non-predatory environment where they can watch, but not partake, of the wonders of our native wildlife." I took this up with my two elderly, sleep-addicted felines, who retired from hunting, or indeed, exercise of any kind, some time ago but still enjoy snoozing in the garden and being outside in the good weather. Their response was non-vocal, but the looks they gave me could, I think, be translated as, "That's for the birds!"

CATS

I t seems that everyone who ever put a pen to paper eventually gets around to writing about cats. In view of my long association with felines, I see no reason to fight this tradition, and perhaps take the opportunity to debunk some popular theories. The first being that cats inspire everybody with either rabid devotion or complete repugnance. I personally held that view until I once heard a woman remark, "I don't care much for cats. Of course, I wouldn't hurt one." I consider that the height of tolerance.

Then there is the generally accepted idea that all cats are utterly independent creatures that hold humans in disdain. Proof that this is false is a tiger-striped female named Cleo who lives with me. Instead of standing around looking haughty, Cleo hurls herself at anyone sitting down —family member or complete stranger—with the restraint of an affectionate St. Bernard … and demands to be petted. Cleo doesn't give a tinker's dam for reserve or dignity. Her theme song is "Love Me and the World is Mine."

Cleo's daughter, Chloe, a fully grown but small black cat, is timid and flighty … not at all trusting even of me, the one who has been catering to her whims for a long time.

It began when the mother cat, Cleo, first appeared out of the woods behind our house eight years ago. A pitiful sight, she was thin and starving, no doubt abandoned by an unfeeling owner. She was suspicious and scared, but hungrily consumed the food I left for her. Gradually, she came closer to the house to eat and after a few days, appeared accompanied by a tiny black kitten, possibly the only survivor of a litter she may have had in the wilds. With care, both cats happily joined the household.

These two, I hasten to say, have long been spayed. My days of playing midwife and the home-finder for kittens are past. When I had children growing up, however, we often had cats with offspring. I heard someplace that a cat with kittens requires the same amount of work as two additional children. I believe it. If you're a serious cat person, the mother cat has to be let in and out at regular intervals, often at inconvenient times (like three in the morning), fed several extra meals a day and, before the blessed event takes place, provided with suitable maternity accommodations, such as a nice cardboard box lined with soft material.

Unfortunately, even with careful preparation, I find that mother cats tend to be flighty and lose their heads at the first sign of the stork. Unless carefully monitored, they may choose to give birth inside the piano, in the basket of clean laundry or on Grandma's prize antique quilt.

The two cats I now have are completely normal compared with former years when our family seem to hit the jackpot in finding screwball tabbies.

There was Felix, an all-black cat who would stand still in the middle of the room, hunch his back, jump straight up in the air and then run up the drapes with a blood-curdling scream. Felix eventually committed suicide by running directly in front of a moving truck.

Then there was George, a completely yellow cat who contracted jaundice. He then had a nose, paws, tongue, all yellow. The efforts of three vets failed to save George.

Claude was another cat who met misfortune. Not, however, seriously. Claude broke his leg but the vet was able to set it and applied a plaster cast. There was something extremely disconcerting about having a cat stomp around the house like Long John Silver. Claude, I am happy to say, recovered and lived to a ripe old age.

All in all, I admire cats. When I look at Cleo, the one with the insatiable need to be petted, I see a creature who was resourceful enough to survive being abandoned, trusting enough to expose her one remaining kitten, and smart and lucky enough to find the softest touch in the neighborhood.

Not so dumb, these animals.

SORTING THROUGH ONE'S LIFE

September 2, 1999

The other day I bought a paper-shredder. I brought it home, set it up, and gave it a trial run. It works perfectly and it's sort of fun to use. Now, I thought, I have taken the first real step in organizing my existence. Toward dealing with the mountains of paper, the myriad cartons of junk, the endless material contained in a two-story house with large basement and garage that has loomed ominously above me for far too long a time. I shall prove to myself that I can do it.

Big talk!

First of all, there's the fact that neither my late husband nor myself ever threw away anything of sentimental value or personal nature, which means that we accumulated an awesome collection of cards, correspondence, pictures and letters. Not to mention bank stuff, tax stuff, legal papers, books, magazines, boxes of miscellaneous STUFF that must be dealt with.

Since this situation is not unique, a lot has been written about how to proceed. I remembered one article I'd read and, following the recommendations, I set up three cartons. Carton No. 1 was for things I would never part with, No. 2 was for throwaways, and No. 3 was for undecided items. Attempting to be cool and objective, I sorted through one box. So far, so good. About an hour later, with pauses for reading over bills and a few letters, I took stock. Cartons No. 1 and No. 3, I found, were nearly full. While No. 2 ,the throwaway box, was nearly empty. So far, nothing had been shredded. And this was just the tip of the iceberg!

The next hour was even worse. I had to seal up the "save" box and set it aside. Then I attempted to reassess the No. 3 box and make decisions. "Ay," as Will Shakespeare would say, "There's the rub." For how can you decide to throw away cards that say what a wonderful wife, mother, grandmother, sister-in-law, or friend you are? Or letters from family and friends when you were away at drama school, or on your own in New York for the first time … or newly married … or having a baby … or moved to the far West and were homesick? Each envelope seemed to bring back a scene from the movie script of my life. They made me chuckle; they made me cry. And they reminded me of something. All too often the pictures of disaster victims searching vainly through the rubble of their homes for some precious remnant—a photo or a scrap of paper to keep and cherish. I felt lucky to have these things in abundance.

I thought of a story I had recently heard about a childless couple who passed away leaving a house and its contents. Their heir, a niece who lived in a distant city, arrived with her husband and they proceeded to clear the decks. When they had left and the property was up for sale, dogs knocked over the rubbish barrels left outside. Good Samaritan neighbors, in an attempt to clean up the mess, were appalled to find among the discards a beautifully framed studio photograph of the deceased couple as well as obviously cherished family pictures and memorabilia of all kinds, including many items about, and a graduation picture of, the heiress niece herself. Remarked one neighbor, "I guess she threw away her life."

I decided not to throw away my life. I'm keeping the photos, and the letters … the Mother's Day cards, the Valentines. Anything that still has meaning for me. I think neatness is highly overrated anyhow.

As for the shredder (I was still looking for something to shred—anything!) I finally came up with some copies of 1980 tax return forms.

They made fine scraps.

Family time. Back row, left to right: Rod, his wife Jan, granddaughters
Laura, Janine and Jennifer. In front: Jerry and Virginia hold great-grand
children Sara and Casey in 1995

PART EIGHT

SALTY AND SPICY

A PRESIDENT IS ONLY HUMAN

August 13, 1998

"Be just and fear not:
Let all the ends thou aim'st at
Be thy country's
Thy God's and truth's"

—*William Shakespeare*

On Nov. 22, 1963, this country suffered a shocking blow. Our young, charismatic, widely loved and respected president had been brutally assassinated. Shot in the head while riding in an open car along a public street lined with cheering crowds, his beautiful wife beside him, to witness the horrible deed, President Kennedy was mourned throughout the world. Investigations and repercussions of this event occupied national and international attention for years and are still ongoing. Honors and memorials to him are legion and his place in history is firmly established.

A case might be made the John Fitzgerald Kennedy was a lucky man. He died a hero. He was never to be hauled up before a panel of inquisitors and face the judgment of millions for his alleged indiscretions ... indiscretions that have been fully described in recent years as including many extramarital affairs, some of them conducted in the White House itself, as well as questionable dealings with underworld figures.

Thirty-five years can make a world of difference. Just imagine what such a confrontation would be like if today's media coverage and public mind-set were employed by a 1963 special investigator. On the hot seat would be not only the chief executive himself, but his brother, Robert, attorney general of the United States. Also, his brother-in-law, and occasional social go-between (to put it politely) Peter Lawford. Also in the witness box would undoubtedly be a frightened Marilyn Monroe, sans makeup and dressed in black, and quite possibly, top Mafia boss

Sam Giancana. And last, but by no means least, one-time buddy Frank Sinatra would have his turn. Talk about a cast! There is a lineup that would make the Starr-Lewinsky-Tripp bunch look like amateur night at the local pub. And if a dress were to be introduced as evidence, let it be the one that Marilyn had to be sewed into to sing "Happy Birthday, Mr. President."

But, you may say, in this hypothetical scenario, President Kennedy couldn't be accused of lying about his affairs under oath. Possibly not. But personally, I find it difficult to imagine him owning up to any of this hank-panky, or for that matter, a procedure of this kind, carrying, as it does, a whiff of a McCarthy witch hunt, even being considered. To my mind, it's beyond belief that it's happening now.

None of this, of course, is meant to take anything away from the martyred Kennedys, John and Robert. Both were really heroes, and so, I maintain, is any individual who comes forth from the crowd and stands up for something ... especially those who are willing to take the heat that comes with public office, the slings and arrows of public scrutiny, both the adulation and the scorn. And some have given their lives.

Besides John Kennedy, Presidents Lincoln, Garfield and McKinley, as every schoolchild knows, were all assassinated. Franklin Delano Roosevelt, although not murdered, nonetheless gave the last ounce of his strength serving twelve years in office during some of the most stressful eras in our history, the Great Depression and World War II. He succumbed to the strain at the start of his fourth term. Since 1951, a constitutional amendment has limited presidential terms to not more than two, of four-year duration, thus reducing the amount of punishing stress on one man.

In this writer's humble opinion, more laws should be passed to protect the man or woman who holds the most important and stressful post in the world. Who among us, given the ability, the brains, the strength, would really want to take on this awesome responsibility? It is a killer. It calls for almost supernatural wisdom, courage, intellect, self-control and concentration. And yet, we have the guts to expect such a person to be above the human frailties the rest of us share ... to be without sin, if you will, and Superman besides.

In a few days, we will hear from the lips of William Jefferson Clinton his answers to the allegations made against him. He is a man of exceptional intelligence, an effective leader, and one who, in spite of unprecedented attack, has so far kept his cool. May he so continue and be allowed to get on with the business for which he was elected.

And may we all reconsider just how far into the private life of any individual we are willing to probe in this free country.

COMMON SENSE ABOUT
GUN CONTROL

May 18, 2000

This is a good time to be female. Today, I am proud to be a woman. To be a mother. To be able to add my voice to all those who are standing up and saying to members of the National Rifle Association with their bullying gun lobbyists and to the elected officials who are under their thumbs, "We have had enough!"

As I am writing this piece, thousands of women are gathering in the nation's capital and here in Rhode Island in Waterplace Park in a demonstration of their support for more effective gun-control measures. It is the beginning of a grassroots movement called the Million Mom March. The movement is a call for women to declare their unwillingness to allow unlicensed and uncontrolled proliferation of firearms, which have resulted in countless tragedies. To make it clear to our representatives in Washington and in every state that we mean business, especially when we go to the voting booth.

For many years, the efforts of members of Congress, who have tried to bring about reasonable legislation to make gun owners more responsible and create a safer environment, have met with iron opposition from those who see any kind of control of firearms as a threat. And these people have relied on the myth, much touted by the powerful National Rifle Association, that the Second Amendment to the U.S. Constitution means that "the right of the people to keep and bear arms shall not be infringed" applies to anyone, ignoring the qualifying first part of the amendment. That qualifier says, "A well-regulated militia being necessary to the security of a free state." To me, the meaning is crystal clear that the founding fathers meant it to apply to members of the military (the militia) in defense of their country.

Even without that application, however, the framers of the Constitution lived in an age when the common weapon was a musket, a heavy military firearm fired from the shoulder and difficult to reload. They had no way of imagining a "Saturday night special," easily available, in the hands of criminal, a curious child, the mentally unbalanced, or anyone with a grievance or score to settle. They had no way of knowing the grievous harm this so-called "right" would make possible. Nor could they know that unprincipled gun manufacturers and dealers would, without conscience, misuse this addition to the Constitution for profit.

Although this demonstration is occurring on Mother's Day, it is not only mothers but fathers, grandparents, siblings, and everyone connected to the victim who suffer when someone is gunned down or accidentally shot. Every person has a stake in this enterprise. While controlling guns is a highly emotional issue, there comes a time when people have to use common sense to institute order and stability in society. There were, for example, no provisions in the Constitution for owning and operating motor vehicles, which were not yet in existence … When they did appear, it was necessary to draft laws and set up operational procedures to make their use practical. In the same vein, it is now well past the time to set reasonable rules for gun control and give owners the chance to demonstrate their sincerity regarding responsibility and weapon safety.

How can anyone object to the simple demands being made for longer waiting periods and background checks for hand gun owners, registration of all hand guns, safety locks on hand guns and the strenuous enforcement of existing gun laws? When you consider what is at stake … the lives lost, the pain and suffering that have resulted because these measures were not taken, petty delays and inconveniences that may occur when acquiring a weapon seem a small price to pay.

Some legislators have expressed cynicism regarding the possibility of the Mother's Marchers reaching their goals and getting support for their efforts, so entrenched are the minority members of the opposition. Women have heard that song before. They heard it for years before they finally fought their way to the polling places and secured the right to vote. But women are tough and determined and not about to lose this battle for the safety of their children and loved ones.

The emotional appeal of today's demonstration ... with mothers who have lost their children to guns and others who have themselves been victimized all telling their stories on national television ... is good. It is a way of getting the necessary focus on the problem. But the real work will being when women continue their efforts on their home turf ... keeping the heat on those seeking to hold political office and spreading the message that effective gun control can, and will be, achieved.

LAST RIGHTS

October 13, 2005

One May night many years ago, I lay on a cot in my mother's bedroom listening to the labored breathing of her drugged sleep. As each exhalation ended in a long pause, I prayed that it would be her last; an end to her suffering and to that of those of us who loved her.

My mother had been a loving, talented person who sang, played the piano and wrote songs. Now, at 59, she was dying of cancer, and my father and I were keeping our promise not to send her to the hospital.

Several days before, I had fired the nurse who had been caring for my mother. Agonizing as the nurse rigidly observed the rule of a four-hour interval between shots of morphine, I had finally made a desperate call to the doctor. He spoke on the phone to the nurse and told her not to be so inflexible. To me, he said, "Give your mother whatever she needs. Understand? Whatever it takes." But the nurse was adamant and so we parted company and I took over my mother's care.

Before she left, the disapproving nurse showed me how to prepare the injection.

After that, whenever my mother woke up, I tried to distract her, talk to her, hold her hand. But soon the pain would return and I would prepare another shot. I never looked at the clock. Time was irrelevant.

Sensing one day that my father was near the breaking point, I sent him off on some errands, some respite from the painful vigil.

I went to check on my mother. She was awake. I took her hand and she looked at me. Her eyes were clearer than usual. I had to bend down to hear the words.

Can't you give me something," she whispered, "something to make me die?"

I thought my heart had stopped. I couldn't breathe. "Is it … the pain?" I said, stupidly.

"That … and I can't go on this way," she said. "I haven't taken any nourishment."

Drowning, I seized upon this straw. "We can fix that," I said with false heartiness.

"Yes, we can. I'll be right back."

Tear-blinded, I stumbled into the kitchen and began to mix some baby cereal, the only food she could take. Then my glance fell on the vial of morphine: small white pellets to be dissolved and injected. It was nearly full; I had refilled the prescription the day before.

It would be so simple … just put all the pellets in the hypodermic … quick and merciful. "Whatever she needs," the doctor had said.

I couldn't do it. I simply took the cereal in to my mother, and she valiantly swallowed a morsel. Then I gave her the regular shot of morphine and she slipped off to sleep.

Two days later, my mother died, unassisted.

I'm sure that many people would consider that ending clearly to be the right and proper one. I do not. I know that I would act differently today. If my help were requested and it were in my power to save my mother, 48 hours or 48 seconds of agony, I would give it.

I do not believe, however, that such a decision should be left to the discretion of a caregiver but should be the responsibility, the designated will of the sufferer, legally available with the assistance of a qualified and compassionate physician.

At this writing, Oregon is the only state in which this civilized provision has been has been made by the Death with Dignity law, which has been in effect since 1997. It affords terminally ill Oregon citizens the right to obtain from their physicians and use self-administered, legal medications. The act "legalizes physician assisted suicide, but specifically prohibits euthanasia, where a physician or other person directly administers a medication to end another's life." The terminally ill patient must be of sound mind, have been advised of all alternatives, make a written, witnessed request, and have a life expectancy of less than six months as agreed upon by two doctors.

I applaud the legislators and residents of Oregon for having the fortitude and intelligence to pass this law and am among those who are appalled by it being reviewed by the Supreme Court under the leadership of newly appointed Chief Justice John G. Roberts. The case, Gonzalez v. Oregon, has its origin in a directive by Attorney General John Ashcroft in 2001, which threatened that doctors could lose their federal prescription privileges if they followed the Oregon law's procedures. A Federal Appeals Court ruled last year that the attorney general did not have the right to penalize doctors in following the state law. A Supreme Court decision is due in July and will be crucial.

Knowing that we have some measure of control over our dying will give new freedom to living, I believe. Hopefully, before long, every state will have similar merciful options available to its terminally ill and needlessly suffering citizens.

In spite of attacks by the present administration questioning the validity of Oregon's Death with Dignity law, the U.S. Supreme Court upheld the law on Jan. 17, 2006. Legislation to obtain the same right is currently being sought by several other states.

BRITISH ART

October 7, 1999

It appears that the British have done it again. This time, without Paul Revere to spread the alarm, Americans have been invaded by an art display. Entitled "Sensation: Young British Artists from the Saatchi Collection" in the Brooklyn Museum of Art, the show has resulted in demonstrations, threats, and a gigantic brouhaha all around.

Some of the protest stems from animal rights activists who strongly object to art exhibits in the form of dead animals, or parts of them in formaldehyde, being shown ... But by far the greatest outrage is directed at Chris Ofili's depiction of a black Virgin Mary decorated with objects composed of elephant dung and magazine cutouts depicting female private parts. It would seem that artist Ofili, as either a genuine form of artistic expression or a calculated and successful means of getting attention, has found a way to offend just about everybody ... white people, black people, religious people, feminists, art lovers, critics, First Amendment rights protectors, and politicos. Especially New York Mayor, Rudolph Giuliani.

At this writing, the mayor, who is a staunch Roman Catholic, has threatened to shut down the whole museum unless the offensive exhibit is withdrawn. Whether he has the power, let alone the right, to do this, remains uncertain. The uproar has, however, accomplished several things.

It has drawn public attention to the peoples' right to freedom of expression. Also to the difference between funding of such expression, whether through money provided by public taxation or from private sources. Many believe that once funds are given to an organization like the Brooklyn Museum that body should make the decision about what to exhibit. A lot of others subscribe to the theory that it is unreasonable that citizens who shelled out their money should be compelled to swallow their revulsion to what, to them, may be sacrilegious display. And that such exhibits be supported privately. Which brings up the question of who makes those decisions about what is and what is not appropriate.

There have always been shocks coming from the world of literature, painting, dance and theater. Irish playwright Sean O'Casey's play, "The Plow and the Stars," touched off a riot when it was first presented in Dublin in 1926, causing O'Casey to leave for England and never return. James Joyce's cutting-edge novel, "Ulysses," written in 1921, was banned in this country until 1933. In more recent times, comedian and social commentator Lenny Bruce, whose work is now being considered important, was hounded and jailed for using shocking language, commonplace today, in his appearances.

None of this is meant to minimize the real and understandable outrage and pain that people feel about the painting in Brooklyn. As a non-Catholic Christian I also find the idea very offensive. But I think we have to consider what is really happening here. The object in question is just made up of paint and canvas, paper, and some animal dung ... To some, perhaps, an artistic expression ... to others, just some more graffiti. No one is being forced to view it. Shutting down a museum is not the answer.

For centuries, artists have presented paintings of Mary as white, angelic, and remote ... But a portrait, whether ugly or beautiful, cannot really convey spirituality. For me, it is enough that a woman named Mary lived and bore a son named Jesus. That He proved early on to have extraordinary spiritual power and in His short earthly career with a few faithful followers healed, preached to thousands, and sent forth messages of love, forgiveness, and hope. Messages that have influenced the lives of untold numbers of human beings for 2,000 years.

The upset over the Ofili painting will soon be over and it will all become a quaint footnote in the archives of art. But the spiritual concept of Mary, the Virgin Mother, untouched by human hatred or ignorance, will endure for at least another 20 centuries ... or for the existence of mankind.

A WORD WITH A LEGACY OF HATE

July 26, 2007

Since it is constitutionally lawful to use plain language (though not necessarily wise or in good taste), I am going to try to write plainly. Not to be shocking, but because as a writer I am not into playing hide and seek with words in referring to the recent big hoo-ha about former chairman of the board of trustees of Roger Williams University Ralph Papitto's alleged use of what is now called the "n" word, during a meeting of the trustees. A gaff that resulted in the removal of his name from the college's law school and a lot of blather in the local media and public apologies in print and on talk radio.

What I found most intriguing about the whole incident, however, was the assertion, made through Mr. Pappito's public relations consultant, that his client said that he never had heard the racial slur word before and heard it for the first time in a rap song. The vision of the 80-year-old law-school head listening to rap songs on his iPod is a bit of a stretch.

Since the gentleman in question and I are members of the same generation, we undoubtedly have similar memories of how middle class society functioned in those days before World War II. It shouldn't be difficult for him to recall, as I do, that when I was growing up, adults had a whole lexicon of denigrating terms covering those with origins different from their own, melting pot or not. Terms that referred to race, religion, or nation of origin. None of these terms were benign, arising from rancor and ignorance. Words used to express disrespect, disdain, indifference, or even hatred. I never heard them at home, but venturing out into the world, I found many of them commonly used.

Recently, I had a discussion with a friend who insisted the "n" word was no more reprehensible than any of the titles in the put-down designations of other groups.

"What do I care," my friend argued, "if some ignoramus refers to me as dago, for instance. My grandparents came from Italy and I'm not ashamed of it."

"Were they kidnapped from their homeland?" I asked. "Did they come in chains?

Were they bought and sold?"

"Of course not," she said.

"Years later, did it take a cruel bitter war between the states to free them?"

"That was a long time ago," she said.

"Obviously not long enough."

"How long will it be before they forget all that?" she said

"Maybe another hundred years," I said. "Maybe never."

In the present world of wide open communication, the viewer/listener finds him or herself accustomed, like it or not, to hearing explicit sexual language and street talk on every imaginable level, sometimes including the "n" word. Why, then, does the use of that one offensive designation carry such a unique stigma? It is really just a form of the word Negro ... still an ordinary, harmless noun to indicate an individual of a particular generic race of homo sapiens, a member of the human species. Defined in the dictionary as "man as a thinking creature as distinguished from other organisms," as are we all.

Of course, the fault lies with history. In the manner, in the tone, and in the evil with which the word has been associated. And if one word can mean so many things to so many people ... can generate so much hurt and hate, it is a crime to use it. And those who do so deserve whatever censure and penalty our society can impose.

THE "BOYFRIEND"

March 23, 2000

The frequent stories are horrendous. Not a week passes, it seems, without a gut-wrenching article about yet another child rape, abuse, or sexual assault on helpless innocents. Pictures in the paper and on TV of men ... a father, a mother's boyfriend, or a relative in handcuffs being hauled off to jail for an unimaginable crime against a child. And one gigantic question comes to mind ... When all this was going on, WHERE WAS THE MOTHER?

Scarily enough, sometimes she was right there! In the recent case involving an infant whose father is charged with allegedly causing the fracture of 21 of the child's bones, the mother claims she only thought he was "playing rough with the baby since it was born" and didn't know that "its bones were so soft!"

Why didn't she know? She was old enough to have sex, gestate an infant inside her body, bear the child ... and to protect it!

And what about the mother whose 18-month-old baby girl was allegedly brutally raped by her boyfriend? In a televised interview, the grandparents revealed that they had become suspicious when the child appeared to be terrified of males. Didn't that ring a bell with its mother?

In the animal kingdom, maternal care and protection are primal attributes. The female keeps the young safe inside a den, a nest, or some kind of haven until she feels the time is right to gradually introduce them to the world's dangers. Strange males are kept at a distance. Even the father, in some species.

In our case, the father is generally programmed genetically to share the nurturing. In fact, he may surpass his mate in this function. Sadly, not always, however. But what about the "boyfriend"? Since this individual is seldom a boy, nor much of a friend ... a lover or sex partner, more likely, how does he fit into the picture of a single mother with kids? Does he like them? Tolerate them? Feel irritated by them? Wish they weren't there? Take out his frustration on them? Unfortunately, the answer to the last three questions is often in the affirmative. Which brings up a sad picture of a woman caught between her hormonal drive and needs in conflict with her maternal instincts. She doesn't mean to neglect the kids ... but she won't let herself believe bad things about him.

All sorts of lame and ridiculous excuses are presented to try to turn blame away from the boyfriend. "The baby fell and hit its head on a toy." The child is diagnosed as having a broken skull and a lack of nutrition resulting in brain damage and both the mother and her boyfriend are held in custody.

In trying to solve what tragic mistake has brought about this breakdown in society, it is easy to blame it all on the sexual revolution ... The idea that people of either gender are entitled to complete sexual and procreation freedom ... Marriage an outmoded consideration. Couples can join, stay together, or part ... as their fancy dictates. They can also reproduce offspring, which creates a problem. The "free" female is very often left to assume double the responsibility. Often the male has gone on his way. You have to wonder. Which one got liberated?

In the "old days" of wedlock and two-partner homes, there were still instances of dereliction. Did domestic abuse exist? Yes. Were there bad fathers and indifferent mothers? Sometimes. But there were also many more warm loving families and happy, protected children. This, of course, doesn't suggest that we can or should go back to bygone ways. We must always go forward. I believe in and will continue to support women in the fight for progress in every facet of life. Society in general has benefited immeasurably now that women have won the opportunity to use their talents, abilities and intelligence on an equal playing field with men. One thing, however, can never change. One unequal factor. The responsibility that goes along with being a mother.

When it comes to child abuse attributed to men in the home, behind nearly every male is a permissive female. A mother not doing her job of guarding those innocents who have only her to stand between them and danger. Nothing in her life should be as important as that.

ABOUT THE PLEDGE

June 24, 2004

I pledge allegiance to the flag of
the United States of America,
and to the republic for which it stands,
one nation under God, indivisible,
with liberty and justice for all.

This is the allegiance to the flag now recited daily in schools across our country. It's had this form that includes the phrase "under God" since campaigning by the Knights of Columbus, a Catholic organization, and other religious groups prompted then President Dwight Eisenhower to ask Congress to add the words in 1954. It was a time when there was a lot of uneasiness about the Soviets.

From the beginning the newly added wording to the Pledge of Allegiance caused many to protest that it violated the constitutionally mandated separation of church and state. Recently one such protest was brought to court by a father who is an atheist and maintains that the daily recitation with the reference to God is unlawful. His claim was upheld in a lawsuit by the 9th U.S. Circuit Court of Appeals in California in 2003.

The child's parents never married and live apart. By law, however, the mother has the say in her daughter's education and, as a Christian, her choice was that the child continue to include the phrase "under God" in her daily pledge. The matter was subsequently brought to the Supreme Court for a decision.

It was an election year, which says a good deal about the way public forums, even at the highest level, are conducted. Members of that august body tap-danced around the hot potato issue with nimble agility that would make Fred Astaire look clumsy, resulting in a temporary ruling, but no actual resolution. Opinions were expressed, but no absolute decision, which leaves a politically volatile issue off the table for now.

Eight justices considered the case and all agreed that the California ruling was incorrect. The reason being that the child's father, who is an emergency room physician as well as a lawyer who pleaded his own case, lacked standing as a plaintiff. This was apparently due to the couple's unmarried status and because under California law the mother has custody. Not having a plaintiff with standing, they said, the federal court didn't have jurisdiction over the case.

The only three justices who expressed their views on inclusion of the "under God" phrase added to the pledge half a century ago were Justices Sandra Day O'Connor, Justice William H. Rehnquist and Clarence Thomas. All said it was constitutional.

Justice O'Connor called the added phrase permissible as "ceremonial deism" rather than religious worship. Chief Justice Rehnquist said that "Reciting the pledge or listening to others recite it is a patriotic exercise, not a religious one."

For both of them, I have a little story told me by a friend who was formerly an elementary school teacher.

One morning, while the class was standing and reciting their pledge as usual, she noticed that when she came to the phrase "under God" one little girl crossed herself. As days went by, other kids, noticing the gesture, began to emulate her. Soon, thinking it must be a cool thing to do and maybe was expected, half the students, including several who were Jewish, were reciting the Pledge of Allegiance and making the sign of the cross.

The teacher explained to them that it wasn't necessary or really appropriate but left it at that.

So much for ceremonial deism and patriotic exercise.

MARS

February 5, 2004

Do you want to go to Mars?

Do you want to send your great-great-great-great-grandchildren to Mars?

Are you OK with billions of American dollars being spent on this enterprise?

How interesting do you find the bleak, dead, surface of a planet millions of miles from earth? Whether or not it once had water that supported some kind of life?

Would you like to have the money it will require used to return to the moon and set up a kind of jumping-off place for future manned expeditions to Mars? Or would you prefer to see those billions of dollars spent in restoring some kind of sanity to planet Earth? To feed starving people, to educate, to set up a health care program, to save our already savaged environment?

I am sure that there are those who view the advancement of scientific projects as a priority. But there are others, I'm sure, who like myself think we have more pressing problems saving the human race from becoming an extinct species. From destroying our own kind with senseless wars and lack of communication between nations, races, religions, cultures, and general misunderstanding. How can we be smart enough to explore far distant planets, when we can't get answers to these basis quandaries that threaten our very existence?

Among members of the scientific community, the very idea of not going forward with further exploration is unthinkable. And they have a point. In the rapid development of man's capacity to decipher secrets of the universe, so much intelligence, energy, and work has been expended.

And it is against all realistic expectations to think anything can stop further progress in those fields.

The trouble with this reality is that the results of science can be beneficial to mankind ... or devastating. Science may one day find a cure for cancer but it has already unlocked the door to cloning. Perhaps not to humans yet, but that cannot be far behind. We have worldwide communication but are still developing more deadly weapons.

If we one day become successful in colonizing Mars will we bring with us our primitive passions and our capacity for war and self-destruction?

It would seem that humanity would be better served by putting more concentration, focus, intelligence and money on solving problems here on Earth than on going to Mars.

A SCARY RUN-IN
WITH ROAD RAGE

September 14, 2003

There is not in nature
A thing that makes a man so deform'd,
So beastly,
As doth intemperate anger.

—*Webster's Duchess of Malp*

D o you ever wonder what happened to courtesy and good manners? Not to mention kindness and consideration. Are we all so distraught from the frenzied pace of our days that life consists of taking one shortcut after another between chores and the unremitting demands upon our time and resources? Is this the source of "road rage," or is there another, perhaps more basic, reason deep within? Lots of questions, I'm afraid, but not many answers.

Why, for example, will the average individual who wouldn't dream of pushing in front of you in line at the supermarket, take on a whole different persona behind the wheel of a car? Inside that formidable, weighty vehicle, the driver's more primitive side seems to emerge. Prone to indignation at real or imagined slights by other motorists, he or she can react in ways that are completely unreasonable and dangerous. In the worst cases, deadly. All too often we have seen the tragic results of such episodes. Sometimes the most trivial driving gaffe can provoke unexpected animosity.

I recently witnessed such a response when driving into a post office parking lot. Another car was approaching the entrance at the same time from the opposite direction. Since I arrived at the run a few seconds before the other motorist I turned in first and parked my car. The lot was almost empty and there were spaces aplenty. Nonetheless, the driver of the other car parked close to me and when I turned my head, I was shocked to see on his face an expression of pure hatred and rage. If looks could kill, I would have been history. Somewhat shakily, I got out of my car and went up to the building. A woman from the other car, avoiding my gaze, went inside ahead of me. I glanced back and was alarmed to see the man approaching my parked car. As the post office was about to close I hurried inside to take care of my mailing, and when I got back to my car the other driver was gone. Not, however, before he had left behind a memento of his fury … a long trail of spittle across my windshield!

After I had cleared away the mess, I reflected on what had provoked this repulsive act, and how it might have been prevented. I remembered that although I had reached the turning point sooner, for me it was a left turn. Technically speaking, the other car's right turn would have precedence over mine if we were equally positioned. How much better would it have been had I waited a few seconds and let him turn first. It had been a split-second call and perhaps I blew it. But how did such a low-key mistake bring forth so much instant rage and desire for retribution?

It would seem that for whatever reasons, a deep build-up of frustration and unresolved grievances lie beneath the everyday façade of many people. They believe that somehow they have been misused by society and by life and secretly feel the world owes them an apology. In his play, "A Thousand Clowns," the author, Herb Gardner, addresses this problem by having a character describe walking among crowds on the streets, saying "I'm sorry" or "So sorry" at random. People's responses almost always being a forgiving, "That's OK" or "That's all right" … eager are they to receive an apology for even a nonexistent offense. So in my haste to get to the post office before it closed, if I was impatient, I offer my apology to that other driver.

I am sorry that I had so little patience … And that you had so little class!

A vehicle can be a wonderful convenience, a source of pleasure and pride. Or it can be a weapon, as deadly as any gun. As opponents of gun control are fond of saying, guns don't kill people, people do—so cars don't kill and maim people, rotten drivers do. And just as we strive to keep guns out of the hands of the immature, the criminal and the unbalanced, we fervently hope to keep car controls out of the hands of the drunks, substance abusers, the hotheads and the loonies.

SO LONG, BILL

December 14, 2000

The tenure of William Jefferson Clinton as president of the United States will soon be over ... and I miss him already.

I realize that many people do not share my feelings and are eagerly looking forward to his departure from the White House. In my view, we may all look back upon the past eight years as the "good times" and President Clinton's administration as an era when we had a man in Washington who was outstandingly intelligent. Clinton had a rare gift for articulation and diplomacy who was able to deal with warring factions from abroad with delicacy while keeping his cool to a remarkable degree with a hostile Congress, and an unbelievable public attack and invasion of privacy.

Bill Clinton is far from being a saint. He had at least one disastrous extramarital affair and probably more during his career. That, I believe, is a matter between his marriage partner and himself, no business of yours and mine. And as for those who voice objections on religious and moral grounds, they should remember the master's words, "Let him among you who is without sin cast the first stone."

Clinton may be no saint ... but neither were Presidents Jefferson, Eisenhower, Franklin Roosevelt, or Kennedy, all of whom reportedly had scandalous involvements with women that, fortunately for them, were not made public during their lifetimes.

Clinton's lying under oath about his indiscretion was a mistake, one that he survived in spite of all the self-seeking, self-righteous, vindictive enemies and voyeuristic media coverage. He somehow managed to put aside public humiliation, and what must have been a private hell ... to keep doing his job, surely the most important and stressful on Earth, with astonishing good grace and dignity. When all is said and done, I believe that he has emerged as an imperfect man, but a good president.

It would be nice if we could have Superman for our president and leader of the free world. Unfortunately, however, we are stuck with choosing a human, faulted very much as we are ourselves. And we have recently had a tough time doing that. Trying to pick candidates without detectable evidence of past transgressions. Ones who appear to be honest, sincere, presentable, loyal, able to talk, walk, smile, hoist infants in the air, look like real down-to-earth folks while having at least a minimal grasp of the current state of the world and our domestic problems. Having chosen three persons who arguable fit these criteria, we then went to the polls across our land and cast our votes ... and we all know how that went!

By the time this piece reaches print, the big question of who won the election may be solved. The situation has become extremely tense and many don't care anymore about who the winner is as long as it's all over. We know that there will be problems ahead for whoever comes out on top. Being a world leader comes with a great price.

As for Bill Clinton, his future looks bright. He will no doubt be in great demand as a writer and speaker here at home, and perhaps as a mediator among countries around the world where there are opportunities for him to use his intellect and understanding of global conditions.

As to the present uncertain situation we citizens find ourselves in ... it soon will be resolved and we will hear a desperate appeal for coming together, for unification after our time of trial. The upside of the unfortunate mess is that we have all had a mass cramming of education about the laws and procedures that govern our country, which can't help making us a more informed electorate.

Let us wish the best of luck to the new president, whoever he may be ... He will surely need the patience and support of all Americans.

P.S. Seven years later, as I am writing this, what can I say? Patience and support did not do the trick? Both have just about run out for President Bush and his administration.

Let's make sure we do better in 2008.

PART NINE

REALLY TART

THOUGHTS OF SURVIVAL

April 19, 2001

The musicians are all in their appointed places, their instruments in hand. The conductor stands at the podium, baton raised; the audience sits in tense anticipation waiting for the downbeat and the music to begin. That is what I felt driving home through the country recently, looking at the still leafless tress, the fields not yet green, the birds returning from their winter journey … the whole world watching for the signal from nature that will once again usher in the miracle of spring.

This is the waiting time, a mini-season between retreating winter and the incoming rebirth. Only a short time ago, we were treated to a breathtaking spectacle. A winter-end snowfall of great beauty with puffy white flakes covering the ground and clinging to every branch and twig like cotton decorations at Christmas time. Then, magically, it all vanished with the appearance of the sun—followed by rain. Soon, the scene here in New England will be a panorama of green as trees unfurl their leaves, yellow forsythia and daffodils burst into bloom and the many color of tulips, lilacs and flowering fruit trees paint a wondrous picture. Every season has its own glory. How fortunate we are on this planet. How blessed.

We take it all for granted. The sun will rise and set tomorrow; the tides will ebb and flow; the moon will shine and life will go on for the animals, the birds, the forests and us. Hasn't it always been that way? No.

Won't it always be that way? Maybe not.

We tend to forget that our magnificent planet, with its oceans, forests, mountains and lakes, was once a chunk of molten rocks and gases hurtling lifeless through space. Eons passed before the conditions developed that made it possible for life of any kind to develop here. For exactly the right mix of chemicals, minerals, and gases to combine in just the right order to produce an atmosphere for the most primitive organisms to survive.

Billions of years were to pass before the primitive progenitors of our species evolved and, in the last few seconds as ecological time is measured, for man to appear. Man, who in his arrogance and ignorance has it within his power to destroy the delicate accuracy and balance of elements that make life possible here.

The way it all works is described simply and beautifully by the distinguished physician, scientist and author Lewis Thomas, who has written: "The whole earth is alive, all of a piece, one living thing, a creature. It breathes for us and for itself, and what's more it regulates the breathing with exquisite precision. The oxygen in the air is not placed there at random, any old way; it is maintained at precisely the optimal concentration for the place to be livable. A few percentage points more than the present level and forests would burst into flame; a few less and most life would strangle."

He goes on to describe that the corresponding levels of other elements like carbon dioxide and methane also are held steady at the right concentration for keeping the earth's temperature and the heat of the oceans exactly right. He speaks of the importance of the greenhouse effect and says, "Statesmen must keep a close eye on the numbers these days ... we are already pushing up the level of CO2 by burning too much fuel and cutting too much forest, and the earth may be in for a climatic catastrophe within the next century."

Thomas wrote these words in 1986, adding his warning to that of countless other scientists and experts as well as that of ordinary citizens who are aware of what can result from the unbridled abuse of our environment. And now, in 2001, we are facing a crisis that none of us can afford to ignore. There are those in charge of our country who appear to be putting the welfare of the entire planet in serious jeopardy.

In this category, the recent decisions made by President Bush to abandon his campaign pledges on environmental issues to curtail power plants' dioxide emissions, his using the excuse of energy shortages to reverse bans on road building and logging in the nation's federal forestland as well as backing drilling in an Artic National Wildlife Refuge are danger signs that his policies can lead to disaster for the future world.

Even worse is his decision to put economic goals ahead of countering the threat of global warming as agreed upon by the United States and most of the world's great powers in Kyoto, Japan, in 1997. His action is inexcusable coming from our country, the planet's leading polluter.

It's time we all realized that environmental issues are not political issues. They mean our survival.

A CALL TO REASON ... NOT ARMS

October 4, 2001

In this column, which has appeared more or less regularly every other week since the South County Independent first began ten years ago, I have been given the freedom to comment on whatever I wished ... sometimes about current affairs ... often an essay or short personal story or a chance to express an opinion or two. I've always enjoyed the opportunity to mull over possible subjects and pick one to write about. In this uniquely distressing time, however, there seems to be no way to ignore what is on all our minds. There it sits ... the 800-pound gorilla ... the ugly intruder in our midst ... the specter of war.

On Sept. 11 of this year an unbelievable thing occurred. Our safe, comfortable (for many of us) world was invaded by horror beyond imagination. Death and destruction of thousands of innocent people ... in the air traveling to vacation spots, business appointments, visits with friends and family. On the ground people working in offices, at their desks, planning, laughing, talking on phones ... all gone in a few catastrophic moments of explosion and fire. And later came the fatal casualties of those heroic police, firemen and workers who rushed to effect a rescue. We are all shaken to the core. How could such a thing happen here, we ask ourselves? How could they hate us that much? And what shall we do now?

Our president has pronounced it a call to war. War against terrorism ... and against all those who plan to take part in it and those countries that support or harbor terrorists.

Surely, there is justification for this response and we all feel like rallying to the cause. But war can have many interpretations. In this case, it can mean searching for and stamping out nests of terrorist activity through the combined intelligence arms of supportive countries and using every diplomatic tool, calling in every marker, using the maximum skills of our government brain pool. Or it can mean raining down destruction on people who are already suffering and impoverished under a cruel dictatorship in a barren land. And it can mean sending our young men and women on yet another killing mission from which many will not return. Such an action could also set off the powder keg of the Middle East and the Arab world in ways terrible to contemplate.

Our problems with that part of the world are complicated and some self-made. We have supported dictatorships because of our foolish dependence on acquiring their oil. We have grossly underestimated the desperation of the region's young men …Those without hope for a future have been easily manipulated by the likes of Osama bin Laden, who uses distorted interpretations of Islam to enlist them in campaigns against the United States. In this indoctrination, they are trained to see any sacrifice as holy, to be rewarded in another life.

In a recent editorial in this paper, the writer, whose work I have always admired, deplored the apparent lack of enthusiasm among American young people to be ready to "serve their country" in whatever capacity is required. Can it be that today's youth sees beyond the historical concept of "serving" enough to hope for more intelligent and ingenious solving of world problems than would involve a body count?

Quoted in the article were the famous words of the American Revolution patriot Nathan Hale, who before being hung by the British, said, "I only regret that I have but one life to give for my country." In all probability, the 19 young Arab men who perpetrated the horrors on Sept. 11, and who perished along with the innocent plane passengers, shared the same sentiment.

In this country, where we have enjoyed freedom and many of us have prospered, we have been given a soul-shaking wake-up call. We now have proof that we are vulnerable and must do everything possible to make life safe again. And doing this involves looking beyond our own doorstep. It means re-thinking social problems here at home … in a land where many children still go to bed hungry and elderly people lack money for food and medical care. It means electing people to high office who are not pawns of the corporate world. It means fighting racism and discrimination. And it surely means seeing ourselves through the eyes of the rest of the world and changing America's image into what we really intend it to be.

TIME TO PURSUE PEACE, NOT WAR (TEXAS STYLE)

October 18, 2001

The man on the TV was talkin' tough. The man was making sure we all knew he was The Man! The man from Texas, who had mispronounced nuclear, calling it "nucular" for the umpteenth time, was there to try to whip us all into a frenzy as he once more made an attempt to link the horrendous attacks of Sept. 11 to Iraq and focus our attention on his main objective: war.

Sure, he has had some temporary restraints attached to his efforts by the U.N. qualifying agreement, but the overall boosts he received from the recent Republican gains in Congress and the U.N. Security Council's unanimously passing a resolution calling for Hussein to disarm or face the consequences gave him extra confidence ... and he pulled no punches.

"We will not forget the harm that was done to us. We will not be distracted from the task before us. No enemy that threatens our security or endangers our people will escape the patient justice and the overwhelming power of the United States of America," Mr. Bush said, during Veterans Day ceremonies at Arlington National Cemetery, his words better fitting the recent terrorist attacks but aimed also toward Iraq.

John Wayne would have loved him. The trouble is, John Wayne was never the leader of the most powerful nation on earth, thank God, and George W. Bush is. Both of them, in their own ways, have played the role of cowboy. Wayne, a college football player turned actor; Bush, son of a president, himself an oil man and rancher, rising quite admirably to denounce the abominable acts committed against our country on Sept. 11 and declaring war on the perpetrators, wherever they might be. Unfortunately, however, the president's agenda has as its primary focus another war, one against Iraq, one in which there can be no happy movie ending and no Wayne-like hero.

As this is being written, the U.N.-approved weapons inspection team, headed by Swedish chief inspector Hans Blix, is en route to Baghdad to begin its work on Nov. 27. Theirs is a daunting and crucial task. Everything depends on them getting unlimited access to Saddam Hussein's weapon stores and, most importantly, making judgments about what is and what is not total cooperation from the Iraqis.

It is said that it is a nearly impossible job ... trouble if they do find weapons, and trouble if they don't.

Blix has stated, "We would like to go through it in such a way that war is avoided. However, war and peace are not in our hands."

Which brings the question, whose hands are they in?

Some of us may feel that there is more to fear from Washington than from Baghdad. Are there enough hawks and Bush supporters just waiting to seize upon the tiniest implied infraction of the rules to launch a war? I think that the president and his advisers should wake up to the fact that the majority of Americans do not want another war! We do not want our young men fighting, killing and dying in the streets of any country. Nor our bombs dropped on innocent civilians.

So what about weapons of mass destruction in enemy hands? Unfortunately, many nations now have them or soon will. And the United States' store of this devastating weaponry vastly surpasses the sum of all the others put together. Are we, being the "good guys," prepared to go around the world deciding who are the "bad guys" and divesting them of their arms?

We should remember that it was the United States that opened up that can of worms in the first place. We are the ones who let loose the evil nuclear genie from the bottle, done with the desperate purpose of bringing World War II to an end, which it did at great cost to all of humanity. It might be said that responsibility for dealing with the outcome rests heavily on our nation, to bring the same concentration of scientific brilliance and dedication that developed this monstrous weaponry to bear on finding ways to peacefully resolve the world's differences. Clearly, massive killing is not the answer.

The fate of Iraq should not depend on the decisions of President Bush alone. It is up to all of us who disagree with his strategy of invasion to write letters, make phone calls, send e-mail and protest to try to prevent this potentially on-going nightmare from happening.

CONFIDENCE MISPLACED?

March 13, 2003

Colin, Colin, what have you done?

Many of us who looked to you as a sane, strong, statesman-like figure who could rein in the dogs of war feel betrayed by your caving in to administration pressure and joining in the attempt to make a case for our invasion of a country that has not attacked us.

You have made a case, spotty though it may be, that there is some reason to think (without any concrete evidence) that: A. There may be hidden weaponry of a destructive nature someplace in Iraq. B. That there may be some terrorists hiding there and plotting evil things…as there are in many other countries. C. That we should be alert, aware of danger, both here and abroad and root out terrorists.

What you haven't said, in all the meticulously prepared address, is that you (and the rest of Americans) will be following a murderous path led by an obsessed president into a quagmire of madness in which the massacre of thousands will stain the American conscience for years to come.

Baghdad is not a small isolated town … It is a city the size of Paris … teeming with people. Mothers and fathers, children, babies, and old people. The beginning of the assault on the country has been said to be a massive bombing with perhaps 100,000 casualties. How can we justify this terrible crime? By the suspicion that maybe Iraq might try to harm us? And with this pre-emptive premise being established, will China feel it will be O.K. to invade Taiwan? Pakistan be justified in using its nuclear weapons against India? What horrors will this insanity let loose on the world?

We will end up being ashamed in our hearts and spirits that we allowed this fiasco to happen. How can we live with the knowledge that the image we all held of the "rightness" of America is a myth only just re-emerging from the stark "wrongness" of what took place in Vietnam?

A few reading this were, like me, around during the days of World War II. No matter how pacifistic you were then, you had incentive and moral imperative to support and aid your country. We had been grossly attacked by a specific country and were justified in every way to feel patriotic and proud of our armed forces. The situation we now confront is vastly different.

What moral ground have we to take such a stand? And what about that of the United Nations? If that body and its Security Council are to have any reason to exist, it cannot be ignored and dismissed by the arrogance of one man, the president of the United states, who holds far too much power.

Where do the majority of Americans stand on these issues? Have we anything to say about what may soon take place? Some are protesting vigorously as are a few of our people in Congress. But many are confused by conflicting feelings of loyalty to their country and convinced by the vague claims of those who would pair Iraq with what took place on Sept. 11.

It is easier to look into the TV screen at the down-home face and hear the voice of the man from Texas and see a patriot who has our best interests at heart instead of a monomaniac who is leading us into a disaster.

By any standard that this country has chosen to live by, there is no honor in this enterprise. It defies every principle we hold. If we let this happen, the words in our national anthem, "The land of the free and the home of the brave" will forever have a hollow ring ... and a bad taste will be left in the mouths of those who come after us.

A SITE OF SADNESS ON
A SPRING DAY

March 27, 2003

This morning, it appears that the spring season that we have hoped and yearned for during this long cold winter is really here.

Tree buds are swelling, the earth is beginning to thaw and when I pushed aside the leaves along the path by my front door, I saw the tips of flower bulbs poking up through the soil, all alive and ready to bring forth daffodils and tulips and crocus blossoms to bring us cheer. And not a minute too soon.

I felt once again that rush of joy that comes with the renewal of life that nature gives to us each spring season, especially welcome after the tragedies of the recent past weeks. Then I looked up from the ground to the twisted limbs of the giant wisteria vine that grows over the porch and saw a sad sight – a small American flag hanging from the branches. The former tenants must have placed it there, possibly after the Sept. 11 event. I have paid it little attention as I have come and gone, usually carrying groceries or hurrying to get out of the snow and cold. Today, the little flag was drooping and looked forlorn.

It looked as though it was saddened by what may be going on in its name, somewhere in the world.

I realize that this may sound overly sentimental and even unpatriotic to some folks reading this. But I know there are many others who will understand.

We all grew up learning great respect for the Stars and Stripes and what they stand for. I have owned flags most of my adult life. Flags of all sizes. I have flown them with pride over my front door on the Fourth of July every year. But this sad little flag brought a lump to my throat. I considered taking it down, rolling it up and carefully putting it away until the day comes when it can once again fly with pride.

Our country is and has been great, not because of wealth or power but because of its values. Most of us hold a firm image in our minds and hearts of what America stands for.

Words like liberty, fair play, justice—all the qualities and ideals we associate with the nation for which the flag is a symbol. Ideals that, to many of us, are now in jeopardy.

As this is being written, a war is in progress. A war that a large number of patriotic Americans find unjustified and unprovoked by the invaded country. In short, a country that has not attacked us and has not, no matter how hard the present administration has tried to make the implication, been responsible for what happened on Sept. 11. Instead, the attack on Iraq is part of a strategy long planned by a group of hawk-like plotters who surround the president. In George W. Bush they found the ideal leader to implement their plans and seized upon the tragedy of Sept. 11 to convince him of their legitimacy.

Even beyond the gravity of what may yet happen to many of our brave service men and women, as well as innocent Iraqis, is the question of what the plotters have in mind for the post-war era in the Middle East. With the United States firmly in a position of power, will we be able to erase the concept of American imperialism? Will the present administration reach out to try to mend the damage done to our relationship with the United Nations? Their help will be sorely needed to aid Iraq in reconstituting its government and especially with humanitarian issues. Or are there other intrusive moves planned by those close to President Bush? The world's oil, of course, is on many people's minds and many of those people are part of the administration. The idea of turning the areas' Muslim countries into Western-style democracies is deemed by many who know that part of the world a fantasy. How many of our resources would be expended in that vain effort?

We are in this quagmire now. It remains to be seen how much trouble we will cause to happen, as well as how much good we will do. If Saddam Hussein is gone, that much will, at least, be a big plus.

Whether or not it will be worth the cost, only time, and lots of it, will tell.

THE STATESMAN

April 4, 2003

George W. Bush sealed my opinion of his mentality with his outrageous attempt to rouse public approval for his completely unjustified plans to send our military forces against Iraq in his speech at the press conference held on March 6. The president once again tried to link Iraq to the Sept. 11 attacks, attempted to preempt the report by Hans Blix about the progress being made in the inspection process, and blatantly promised that whatever the vote came from the United Nations about the action, it would not deter him from "disarming Saddam."

Speaking in a studied calm manner (no doubt having been warned by his advisers to tone down the belligerence) he stated, "I will not leave the American people at the mercy of the Iraqi dictator and his weapons."

Do we have an Iraqi dictator with weapons on our borders? Or do we have an American dictator, and an obsessed one at that, in charge of our lives, the lives of our sons and daughters, the honor of our country, and possibly world stability? We had better take the blinders off and see him for what he really is. A man fanatically dedicated to finishing the job his father left undone, getting a grip on Middle East oil supplies, and imposing his idea of democracy, a concept dangerously close to imperialism, on the whole region. A kind of global Hannibal Lecter intent on gobbling up whatever is available. In his words to the press, the president attempted to ring in all possible support by hitting the "faith" button. "My faith sustains me because I pray daily," he said. He would pray for the troops, he added, as well as for innocent Iraqi lives. I found this ploy especially egregious in light of what his plans would undoubtedly mean for those unfortunates on both sides.

Playing the religion card is probably the most dangerous note to strike in this confrontation that involves a mostly Christian-grounded country about to invade a largely Muslim section of the world. Another Crusade, it becomes obvious to the people of the Middle East, thereby strengthening their resistance to any idea of democracy a thousand-fold. This tactic alone reveals the absence of perception and plain common sense on the part of George W. Bush.

He has, so far, managed to defy and insult the other world powers, except Great Britain, ignore Congress, and insist that his will and his alone will prevail regarding the invasion of the Middle East. All the while, his focus is on Iraq, which at least for the present does not have nuclear capability, and brush aside any possible threat from North Korea, which does. Does this sound like the actions of a sane leader?

Meanwhile, our Congress, the men and women we have chosen to speak for us are, it's sad to say, not speaking ... with a few notable exceptions ... Massachusetts Sen. Ted Kennedy has tried to inject some protest, as have a few others. Most are willing to go along with Bush's agenda and looking to protect their own flanks, while hoping for the best, it appears.

Only one man stands out magnificently from this crowd. The senior senator from West Virginia, Robert Byrd, whose speech in the Senate on Feb. 12, 2003, will, I believe, go down as a voice of sanity and states-manship when this whole period is recorded in history. Every thinking citizen should read his words and keep a copy of them to hand down to posterity. I would like to print his entire speech, but of course that is not within my power ... I can, however, quote a few excerpts.

Referring to Congress's inaction, he said, "...This Chamber is, for the most part, silent ... ominously, dreadfully silent. We stand passively mute in the United States Senate, paralyzed by our own uncertainty, seemingly stunned by the sheer turmoil of events."

"This administration," Senator Byrd stated, "has split traditional alliances, possibly crippling, for all time, international order-keeping entities like the United Nations and NATO. This administration has called into question the traditional worldwide perception of the United States as well-intentioned peacekeeper."

In his closing paragraph, the Senator said, "I truly must question the judgment of any president who can say that a massive attack on a nation which is over 50 percent children is 'in the highest moral traditions of our country'. This war is not necessary at this time."

His words ring true for me … and I believe for a great many more Americans.

THANKSGIVING IN IRAQ

December 4, 2003

In the enduring hit musical and recent motion picture "Chicago," one of the characters, Billy Flynn, a lawyer best known for his flamboyant and questionable tactics in winning in court, tells a client how it's done by singing his big number, "Razzle Dazzle 'Em." I was reminded of this when the picture of President Bush, standing in the heavily guarded Baghdad International Airport, wearing a jacket with a large ARMY insignia and holding a platter of turkey, appeared on all media outlets the day after Thanksgiving. During his two-and-a-half-hour stay, the article caption said, the president assured the cheering soldiers that America stands behind them.

No doubt this dramatic and well-kept secret appearance of Mr. Bush was orchestrated by the same team of backstage managers who arranged the president's visit, in a flight suit, aboard an aircraft carrier a short time ago. Another magnet for photo media. Those big-time producers, Cheney, Rove, Rumsfeld, and the rest, must know all the lyrics to the song. When the natives seem to be getting restless, tired of being lied to, and anxious to see some light at the end of this dark tunnel of deception, they get the president into appropriate military attire and send him out with a rousing chorus of "Give 'em the old razzle dazzle, razzle dazzle 'em."

Apparently, they haven't yet caught on to the fact that the majority of Americans haven't just fallen off the old turnip truck and are not impressed. Neither, by all accounts, are the Iraqis. Opinions about the event made by the locals, according to Associated Press reports, were that Bush used the two-hour visit to impress the voters back home, "He came for the sake of the elections," said one man. "He never thought of the Iraqi people. He doesn't care about us." Religious leaders, at prayers in the mosques, also spoke out against the president's two-hour touchdown in Baghdad. "Mr. Bush should spend his energy helping Iraq recover from the war, not on flying across the world to pose for the cameras," said an Iraqi imam.

The 600 soldiers from the 1st Armored Division and the 82nd Airborne who were on hand for the holiday meal were, naturally, overwhelmed when the surprise visitor, their president, leader of the armed forces of the United States, suddenly appeared before them. They gave him a rousing welcome, cheering, climbing on chairs to welcome him … applause, applause. Just like show biz.

After that, it was back to the Humvees, back to the Black Hawks…back to the dangerous streets of Baghdad. Back to being hated by many, unwanted by a people who, they had been told, would welcome them as liberators but who consider them invaders. The Americans are intruders into their country and their culture. They are bunglers who seem to have no clue about getting their own act together, let alone helping them get together their act.

In the last thirty days, our forces in Iraq have lost 83 men and women in the war, the greatest number in any one month. This includes six Americans who died in an Air Force plane that crashed in Afghanistan. According to the Pentagon, 2,094 American troops have also been wounded in Iraq so far. In view of the heavy price our young service members and their families back home are paying for this ill-advised debacle, President Bush's 150 minutes inside the 15-square-mile, heavily-guarded Baghdad Airport, appears to many to be a self-serving expensive ploy to curry favor back in the United States.

We have been repeatedly misled and lied to by the present administration … by the insinuation that somehow Iraq was involved in the Sept. 11 attacks … about the existence of weapons of mass destruction in Iraq … by selling us the idea that with our superior forces, we could bring in a brand of democracy that would be instantly adopted by a country with a vastly different historical, cultural and religious background. And that we could do this alone while thumbing our noses at the United Nations and the rest of the world.

Now, the bad planning of the program by the administration is becoming glaringly apparent. Our people who are in the danger zones are becoming targets for attack by Iraqis and terrorists from other countries. The formation of a new governing body made up of Iraqis hits snag after snag. To put it mildly, things are not going well.

In such times, it is both fitting and ironic to see a picture of George W. Bush holding a turkey.

WOMAN'S FATE A MEDIA CIRCUS

March 21, 2005

By the time this piece goes to print, the sad saga of Terri Schiavo probably will have been resolved, and it is the compassionate hope of many that she will have been released from the nonlife condition in which she has lingered for 15 years.

Terri Schiavo's life really ended in 1990 when her heart stopped briefly from chemical imbalance. Since that moment, the poor woman, although declared brain dead by experts, has been kept alive by means of medical intervention during the tug-of-war between her husband, who claims she would not have wished it, and other family members still desperately hoping for her eventual recovery. It is an anguishing situation for everyone.

The saturation coverage of this event brings up the question of whether we have become addicted to media-supplied focus on issues that arouse primitive emotions, regardless of their relative significance. The Schiavo, case, of course, involves basic elements of our existence, the right to live and the right to die. Both of them, in my view, of equal importance. The unbelievable intrusion into this family's dilemma by everybody, including the president and members of Congress, is mind-boggling, especially the attempted political assault to manipulate the strength of our judicial system, which is where our guarantee of liberty lies.

Sometimes, not being exposed to media can be healthy. I recently spent some time in moving to a new residence and, for several weeks, had no TV or computer access. Talk radio is not my thing, anyhow, and I listened instead to stations that feature classical and swing music. It was like a vacation from the constant bombardment we normally get from media, and I found it rejuvenating.

However, like most people, I wanted to keep up with what's going on in the world and soon was glad to get my remote and tuned in. I wasn't happy to see what I saw: crowds of people protesting the court's decision in the Schiavo case.

It is offensive to all sensibilities to observe the promotion of one unfortunate situation when our military forces are engaged in actions in which many human beings lose their lives every day. To see on TV "news" numbers of people demonstrating in favor of keeping one brain-destroyed individual alive and then pausing for a few seconds to pay tribute to a fallen U.S. soldier, that of a vital, healthy 21-year-old who has just lost his life in Iraq. One of the hundreds now lost, and no end in sight.

Where are the demonstrators to protest this situation?

As we are all aware, the media responds to what it believes the public wants to see, hear and read about. Subjects that get the most intense coverage include celebrity trials, scandals, national disasters and so-called "human interest" stories. Hard news coverage takes a backseat in most instances. We hear about important events, but if it's a choice between Michael Jackson's trial or United Nations news, Michael is sure to win.

The media is controlled by commercial interests that want us to buy their products. We are not forced to watch their programs nor buy their products. So, ultimately, we are to blame. It's our choice if we are manipulated, whether by big industry, politicians or bad judgment in high places—by not seeing behind the smoke-screen saturation of sensationalized non-news stories.

HARD QUESTIONS

April 24, 2005

Onward Christian soldiers,
Marching as to war,
With the cross of Jesus
Going on before.

How many times can you ask, what are we doing over there? What are our young people dying for? What are their people dying for? What shows up? ... Intrusion, delusion, confusion? Is it, at least in part, a religious war? Christian-oriented forces with masked motives invading an overwhelmingly Muslim world? Is it politics, democracy, hypocrisy?

Were we sold a bill of goods after that black day in September of 2001? Casualties of dead and wounded Americans already number in the thousands, with many more Iraqis, men, women, and children dying as well. All under what's being called the "War on Terrorism."

What is terrorism? Human beings hating other human beings. People who are willing, even eager, to give up their own lives to kill those whose religious and cultural beliefs differ from their own. A self-perpetuating evil. It entered our world with the disaster of Sept. 11. And now we must ask ourselves, has it lessened or grown worse since our invasion with bombs and guns and soldiers into the Middle East? Indeed, could not this kind of intervention, in spite of original good intentions, be listed under the heading of terrorism itself?

To eliminate this horrid consideration, let us consider why we went there in the first place. Did the Sept. 11 episode originate in Iraq? No. Did the tyrant Saddam Hussein have weapons of mass destruction? No. Was there any obvious threat from that country to the United States of America? No. Did that country have control of a great deal of oil and present an opportunity to gain a foothold in the whole region? Yes. And were there those in power here in the United States who were still smarting from a previous lost opportunity to do so and eager to remedy the situation? Of course.

And what about bringing the wonders of democratic government to Iraq … and ultimately the whole region? Here is where the assessment of the picture enters the unrealistic twilight zone. Our ideal of democratic rule, which to Americans today incorporates the rights of women and minorities, evolved over centuries going back to England's Magna Carta in 1215. How could the planners of this venture, or any of our people, expect to pull off a quick fix in an ancient world steeped in tradition and adhering to a strict unwavering faith? Especially since the proposition is being delivered accompanied by Christian soldiers (infidels to them) with guns and body armor.

Which brings us to the heart of the whole incongruity. Very few Americans are willing to recognize the significance of the religious involvement that appears glaringly obvious since most of the power of these countries, whether Afghanistan, Iraq, or Iran, appears to be in the hands of Muslim religious leaders, despite elections, political posturing, and maneuvering, but little evidence of real governance.

We must realize that there is not, and probably never will be, any separation of church and state in these countries, like that which came into being with the U.S. Constitution.

Why are we not universally calling for an end to this unrealistic bloody conflict? Demanding that we get out of this NOW! Face the facts that there are elements at work in the Middle East that we cannot fix, regardless of the cost in lives or money

We got rid of the dictator, Saddam Hussein. Now it's up to the Iraqis to form their own government. We must hand them back their dignity, their sovereignty, and the opportunity to make it all work.

And get the hell out!

THE RIGHT THING TO DO

March 30, 2006

I never expected to say this, but I must. I have found an issue upon which I can heartily agree with George W. Bush. I think he's got it right this time. I refer to his proposed program regarding the immigrant problem.

If I understand him correctly, he approves giving the illegals, mostly from Mexico, a break which they heartily deserve, and a chance to remain here where our citizens have long lured them, worked them, and been profoundly grateful to hire them for the jobs that are essential but unwanted by most of our workers. Way to go, Mr. President! Let's keep the people who have been here for decades, in many cases, have their children in schools and receiving some health care while their parents are out there working their hearts out to provide for them. Many of these children were born here and are already citizens.

Now we need to acknowledge these people with something like the "guest worker" status mentioned by Bush, and in the chance to attain future citizenship.

During the past weekend, thousands of demonstrators filled the streets in California and other states to rally for immigrants' rights and protest a federal measure (HR4437) that would make felons of all illegal immigrants, as well as those aiding them and fence a third of the Mexican border. That last proposal might be called for if the government cannot find any other way to contain the in-coming tide. Obviously, it must be stopped ... but the idea of punishing people whose only aim is to latch on to the American dream and have greatly contributed to our way of life, is monstrous.

In a former piece, I wrote about when my husband and I and two boys lived in the San Fernando Valley in California and had a small house with two acres, including a brush-covered hillside. When the annual fire season arrived, roughly late July until the rainy season in November, our hillside property was a disaster waiting to happen, due to the extremely dry conditions and the Santana winds. A law in Los Angeles County demanded that property owners clear the flammable brush 20 feet from a dwelling. We were eager to comply, since we had experienced several close calls from fires. Luckily, when we needed help, a man named Juan showed up at the right time, his truck loaded with a crew of Latino men. Armed with machetes, they tackled the back-breaking work and did a thorough job of clearing the chaparral for a reasonable price. Nobody asked to see their green cards.

Next door to us lived a retired movie actor and his wife. When they both became ill and needed help, a strong dependable Latino woman, Maria, was hired. Maria, who spoke little English, took care of two people, cooked, cleaned, did the laundry and walked two miles to the store and back (until I began driving her) to shop for food.

Once a week, she made the long trip to the barrio of East Los Angeles to bring food and some money to her children. A trip that required a long walk and three bus changes

Nobody inquired into her legal status. She was indispensable.

In nearly every restaurant in Los Angeles, or Southern California, there are dark-complexioned, white-coated figures moving swiftly and efficiently through the kitchens and among the tables, doing the clean-up jobs and whispering in Spanish to one another. Behind the doors of small sweat-shop factories ... In the vast fields of the San Joaquin and Coachella valleys where much of the country's fruits and vegetables are grown and in the lush vineyards of the wine country, they labor ... doing the back-breaking jobs unwanted by the rest of the population. Taking care of the children of career mothers, cleaning their homes, tending the gardens.

The hypocrisy of those who would penalize these people, many of whom have been in this country for years, is mind-boggling. A symbiotic relationship exists between the employers and the Mexican workers, legal and otherwise. If the jobs were not there, they would not come. The two groups need each other to survive.

Luckily, the U.S. Senate Judiciary Committee is scheduled to resume work on a comprehensive immigration reform proposal. The Senate committee's plan, proposed by Senators John McCain (R-Arizona) and

Edward M. Kennedy (D-Massachusetts) embodies parts of various bills, including a guest worker program and a path to legalization for the nation's 10 to 12 million undocumented immigrants.

Let us hope that people who have worked hard and made a contribution will find their faith in this country justified.

During the nearly two years since this piece appeared the U.S. illegal immigration problem has been hashed over interminably from Democratic and Republican viewpoints with no concrete decisions made. My enthusiastic responses about President Bush's early proposals have considerably changed. The whole problem has become a political football. Its proposed solution has become part of every candidate's platform in the 2008 election. Something must be done, but when and how?

PART TEN

JUST DESSERTS

FIRSTS

April 22, 1999

More than a year after Gerry, my husband, died, I went back to California for a family gathering for the first time by myself.

In general, firsts are good. Like the beginning of the new year when, no matter how jaded, we feel we've been given a new opportunity, a new chance to get it right. To stop smoking, to lose weight, to advance a career, to straighten our personal problems, to start meditating ... to get our lives back on track.

They are good even when they're scary. Like the first day in a new school when you feel you're never going to fit in. Or the first time you go looking for a job and feel the chill that comes from stepping out into the real world.

Then there are the great firsts. Falling in love. The first time you have your own place and make it into a home. The first baby being born. And, sadly, there are the painful ones such as I experienced, after a lifetime of splendid firsts. Boarding a plane alone en route to a family celebration of a major holiday without my life's companion.

It seems to be that flying calls for a certain mind-set to endure the unnatural condition of close confinement in a metal box with a crowd of strangers for a lengthy period during which your welfare, and indeed, your life, rest entirely in the hands of others.

Looking around at the other passengers, I wondered how many, like me, are uptight flyers. How many, like me, are going through the trauma of grief that we all inevitably must face in some measure.

I feel a rush of compassion, a realization that we of the human family are bound together by our capacity to give and receive love, as well as by our vulnerability. We are destined to suffer, and yet to deal with, devastating loss. We are all, so to speak, cut from the same cloth.

I can see it on people's faces, in spite of the public masks we all wear as we make our way through the world. That large lady, huffing and puffing as she struggles to get her carry-on bag into the space above her seat. Anxiety turning into relief and gratitude when a man offers to give her a hand. The man himself, looking fit from possibly working out, proud of himself but concealing it with a brief nod as he accepts her thanks.

The young mother with the fussy baby, rummaging through her bag for something to pacify him. Nervously glancing around at her seatmates who seem to be shrinking into their spaces, no doubt thinking this may turn out to be a long trip.

The long trip was immeasurably brightened for me by the young sailor who got on the plane in Chicago, fresh from completing training at the Great Lakes Naval Station. He was on his way to begin his naval career in San Diego and was a perfect poster boy for what Uncle Sam would like to get in any branch of U.S. service. In fact, he embodied the ideal young American … Full of enthusiasm, pride in country, a 19-year-old farm boy from Virginia, who, in his southern drawl, regaled me with stories of home, family, and showed me pictures of his girlfriend, "the sweetest girl you'd ever want to meet, ma'am." That whole scene, the fresh-faced sailor boy showing snapshots of his girlfriend to the elderly lady seated on the plane, would have made a perfect Norman Rockwell cover of *The Saturday Evening Post*.

Arriving at my destination, I find comfort in being enveloped in the warmth of family. Each member, by sharing sorrow, lifts a bit of my burden. My elder son, Gerry, Jr., and his wife, Jan, the two older granddaughters, Jennifer, from Oakland, and Janine, from Carmel, with her two little ones, Sarah, three and a half, and Casey, nearly two, the youngest granddaughter, Laura, a sophomore at UCLA, who shares an apartment near the campus. They all help.

The little ones exulted over the presents I've brought. A doll for Sarah. "Just what I wanted!" she crows, hugging it. A few minutes later, the doll lies tossed in the corner as she is ecstatic over another toy.

Casey is totally absorbed with a set of colorful fitted cups. He explores each one, tracing the patterns with his fingers, building a tower, and finally, pouring water from one to the other. His unbridled imagination searches for the limits of possibilities.

As so it is with me, as well. Searching for answers; learning to survive, dealing with new first each day. And finding that there is much to be hopeful about.

Of course, there is the inevitable family photo session. Everyone gathered around with the picture-taker maneuvering people into position.

"Now, get ready," he warns.

I remember a picture of my own great-grandparents, taken before I was born. A grim New England portrait.

"OK," he says, "now give me a smile, everybody."

I give him a big one.

Years from now, when my descendents come across this picture, I want them to see me smiling.

Left to right: Jeff's wife Betsy, Jeff, myself, great-granddaughter Aiyana and her mother, Jennifer in 2003.

THE ART OF EXPRESSING APPRECIATION

September 28, 2000

The deepest principle in human nature is the craving to be appreciated.
—William James

The day was gloomy and the interior of the small neighborhood variety store rather dark. The middle-aged female clerk leaned disconsolately against the cash register behind the counter and surveyed the few customers unhappily. "This is a low paying, boring job," her look seemed to say, "and I am stuck with it with nothing to look forward to."

I came to her with my purchases, searching inside my purse for money. Suddenly, I realized I'd forgotten to make a stop at the bank and would have to rely on my checkbook. The clerk eyed me balefully as I handed her a check with my identification and I watched admiringly as she began to write down the information.

"What beautiful handwriting you have," I remarked.

She straightened up from the counter and stared at me. "Do you really think so?"

"I certainly do," I said, sincerely. "I only wish that mine were half as good."

A smile spread over her formerly austere features. "My father taught me my penmanship," she said proudly. "He was very particular about it." She went on to tell me about her childhood in Germany, talking warmly about the past and her family, and we parted friends.

When I left the store, I marveled at the change my modest words of praise had brought about in the woman. They had been spontaneous and uncalculated and she had reacted like one who is thirsting for something. Self-worth, perhaps? Approval? I searched for the right word. Appreciation ... that was it!

At home, I looked up the word in the dictionary. "Appreciation: Recognition of the quality, value, significance or magnitude of people or things." Other meanings were "awareness or delicate perception." Something that all of us need and yearn for. Recognition of our qualities, our abilities. I wondered, guiltily, how often I had neglected to give that to others, not realizing how much it meant to them.

"The applause of a single human being is of great consequence," said the famous British essayist, Dr. Samuel Johnson.

I thought of the time some years ago when an essay of mine first appeared in a national publication. It was a piece of nostalgia, telling of my great-aunts and their enjoyment of life and of the things we did together when I was a child. After the first thrill of seeing it in print died down, I wondered how many had read it and if they had gotten anything from it. A week or so later, I received a letter from a doctor in another state that said, in part, "how wonderful to have such memories and to give them to others to enjoy."

That letter meant so much to me at that stage in my writing experience. I read and re-read it many times. I will always be grateful to that busy, kind man who took the time and trouble to give me that feeling of being appreciated.

Wise parents and teachers have always understood the importance of building a child's confidence by acknowledging his or her good qualities and talents, great or small. For both children and adults, such recognition may provide a short-term lift of spirits, last for years, or even change one's life.

Some decades ago, writer Dale Carnegie brought out a book, "How To Win Friends and Influence People." It is still worth reading today, lavish with examples of people whose gift for honest appreciation for others brought them great success in life. He wrote, "The rare individual who honestly satisfies this heart hunger will hold people in the palm of his hand." However, he also counsels that, "The difference between appreciation and flattery is simple. one is sincere, the other, insincere."

It seems to me that the real value of looking for and expressing one's recognition of positive things in other people is two-fold. As in Portia's speech about the quality of mercy in Shakespeare's "The Merchant of

Venice" ... It is twice blessed, it blesses him who gives and him who takes.

A powerful multi-millionaire once made a practice of walking along the streets of New York dispensing dimes to the children. In the same way, freely giving out small tokens of appreciation can make anybody feel as rich as a Rockefeller ... or even Bill Gates!

THOUGHTS ON A COUNTRY CHURCHYARD

June 8, 2000

It is a natural resurrection, an expression of immortality.

—Henry David Thoreau

The months of May and June contain, in their 61 days, the greater part of springtime's significant events. Flowers bloom, trees unfurl their leaves, returning birds build nests and start to raise their families, as do animals both wild and domestic. And in the world of humans it is traditionally the time when many "a young man's (and woman's) fancy turns to thoughts of love" and when many get married ... and when babies are christened, when school and college graduations take place. And when Memorial Day occurs. A time to honor the dead.

Going to the cemetery with pots of flowers to place on the graves of family members, I began to ponder the meaning and relative importance of tradition in this new millennium. Young, and not so young, people have been expressing a lack of interest—in fact rejection—of what was once believed to be customary. And certainly everyone should be free to make choices. Visiting a cemetery—or not—is one of those decisions. It makes no difference to those who lie under the markers in the grassy plots. To visitors, however, the ritual of paying homage and respect to the memory of those who have gone before can bring a sense of fulfillment, of continuity. Saying to those who have preceded them, "I remember. I will never forget you."

In 1938, Thornton Wilder's wonderful play, "Our Town," a simple tale of life, love and death in a small New England town, opened in New York. Surely it remains one of the best American dramas. I was privileged to be in the city at the time and knew some of the people connected with the show. In later years, both my husband and younger son appeared in other productions of the play. I have attended numerous presentations of "Our Town" but always say I will never go see another. I find the beautiful touching scene in the country graveyard so affecting that I make a fool of myself with crying.

I do not find that to be the case in real life when I go, several times a year, to the country cemetery where members of my own family are buried. It is, in actuality, much like the one in "Our Town" might be, with graves dating back to the early 1800s. Big ancient trees—oaks, pines, copper beech and maples—stretch their branches protectively over the stone and marble markers. A calm peaceful feeling seems to prevail. I do not feel sad when I go there. I know that what lies beneath the ground is unimportant. The place is symbolic; it provides a focus for reflection, for memory, and a reminder to live life fully day by day. I leave my offerings in front of a stone in a cemetery where my parents, grandparents, great-grandparents, a great-great-grandmother, great aunts, an aunt, uncle, cousins and my beloved husband lie. I know that one day I will join him there and am content with that. For now, I intend to enjoy being alive.

I go back to the world where chaos often seems to rule and people would like to believe that tradition is worthless—that old customs like marriage, things like fidelity, integrity and age-old rituals that remind us of our tribal past are outmoded. They are welcome to that view … but it makes for a long, cold, lonely trip.

To those people I would say, it really is better to have trust, that marriage is more than having words spoken or written on a "piece of paper." That it's important to have faith and that the old traditions that make us human will never really go out of style.

GOOD TIMES COME
OUT OF STORAGE

July 28, 2005

Since moving into an apartment into which I have been able to bring all of my belongings out of storage, many long unseen items have surfaced, some welcome and others that caused me to question my sanity about having held on to them for so long.

Things like that two-piece silk, beautifully embroidered, Chinese garment that somebody's boyfriend brought back home after World War II. It would probably be a collector's dream except for the fact that a friend wore it to a costume party one Halloween and spilled liquid, causing the colored yarn to run. There it has lain in a plastic garment bag for decades because I haven't brought myself to throw it out.

Then there are several cartons full of very old and very difficult classical piano music portfolios that belonged to my mother and which I have neither the expertise to play nor even a piano to play them on anymore.

There are, in addition, literally several dozen boxes of carefully wrapped individual pieces of china, glassware and bric-a-brac that I would love to distribute among my young women family members ... except that they all happen to live on the West Coast. Getting those items across the country in one piece doesn't seem likely.

Of course, there are also the things I am so happy to get into my hands once again. Especially the books. I have missed having them most of all. There is something about having your own books about you that is immensely gratifying. Even books you have never read and may never fully read. Like the entire 20 volumes of The Nobel Prize Library winners that belonged to my husband's father, a scholarly Oxford man. The volumes are beautifully bound and illustrated. It is a pleasure to pick one up now and then, to hold it, open its pristine pages and read something about or written by a learned individual. Then there is the series of volumes, "The History of Civilization," by Will and Ariel Durant, really heavy stuff in more ways than one. I figure that if I read a few chapters each week, I will eventually feel I've become really educated. Naturally, there is some pretty light stuff as well. Some James Thurber, some plays, lots of poetry and just about all of Will Shakespeare. Not too many modern novels, I'm afraid.

Except I have got "The Perfect Storm" right next to "Moby-Dick." When it comes to books, eclectic is the name of the game.

Much frustration has been associated with a lot of my accumulated stuff over the years. One of the worst cases of this has been a collection of old recordings on 78s that I've had for a long time and not been able to listen to. They were given to my late husband quite a long time ago and we never did get to listen to our favorites from the big band era. They have just stayed there, packed in a large round cookie tin for the past 20 years.

I have lugged the heavy load from place to place, always hoping that someday I would find a way to play these gems. Recordings from the likes of Glenn Miller, Count Basie, Jimmy and Tommy Dorsey, Benny Goodman, Glen Gray, Fats Waller, Xavier Cugat, Woody Herman and Duke Ellington, with vocalists such as Peggy Lee, the Andrews Sisters, Bing Crosby and Connie Haines. Then a wonderful thing happened. Old friends and neighbors, Dan and Kathy Rakosky, from my former home in Usquepaugh, came bearing a gift. From a large container they brought out a beautiful, brand new, mahogany-colored wooden turntable that plays the old records, whether 33s, 45s or 78s! My friends had searched high and low for such an instrument, finally locating a company, Crosley Radio Corp. of Louisville, Kentucky, which manu-factures handsome reproductions of old phonographs, juke boxes and radios, among others. What a blessing!

The old records I have are not perfect, but as a group of old friends listened to the sounds of the 1930s and '40s they seemed like the per-fect blast from the past.

SECONDHAND ROSE

November 29, 2006

The lady in the jewelry store, who had recently been so helpful when I had brought in an antique necklace to be repaired, now looked sympathetically at what I had placed on the counter before her, a small delicate cameo and a gold frame that didn't seem to fit. It had been my hope that, together with a gold chain, it could be a present for a granddaughter's birthday. The repaired necklace had already been given to her sister. These pieces of jewelry, handed down from former generations, were not priceless gems, but represented, to me at least, small parts of family heritage, and I was disappointed when the jeweler found it would be impossible to make the framed cameo work.

Looking around the store, I spotted some consigned antique pieces in one case and after looking them over, selected a fan-shaped pin to send as the gift. I consoled myself with the thought that while the ornament was not a keepsake from my family, it had been part of another's. It had a history, although unknown, and how much difference did it really make?

This episode got me thinking about the whole process of objects being passed from one individual to another, either in the high-toned realm of antiquing and collecting down to the day-to-day world of acquiring used goods, often bearing the euphemistic title of "previously owned." Things change hands, and looking around, I could see that, like the old-time vaudeville Fanny Brice song, I myself was a typical "Secondhand Rose." I drive a formerly owned car, have some antiques, but also some secondhand furniture, and in my closet are a number of clothing items with good labels that were purchased in consignment shops.

By far, however, the most secondhand items show up in my bookcase shelves, where at least half the volumes were formerly owned.

Addicts like me will stop at nothing to extend their holdings beyond capacity.

A few weeks ago, as an example, I had heard there was to be a book sale at a local library and had every intention of culling out a few items from my overstocked shelves. I forgot all about the event, however, until I happened to pass the library in question on a Saturday morning and saw a crowd waiting for the doors to open. Against all better judgment, as soon as they did, I went in … just for curiosity's sake, I thought. About an hour later, I staggered out to my car with two overloaded bags of books and, if I hadn't been exhausted, would have undoubtedly gone back for more.

There is a vast difference, of course, between books and other formerly used items. The importance lies between the pages of the volumes … Tools of communication. Books pass along experience, stories, ideas, inspiration, knowledge. They can stimulate, bring solace, pleasure, or just periods of relaxation and enjoyment. They can answer a quest.

Such an experience took place several years ago when I sold my home. With my son's help, I took some refuse to the Rose Hill Regional Transfer Station in South Kingstown that has a small adjacent building serving as a library for folks to leave free reading material. One of our discards was an old volume, a Machinist's Manual, which had belonged to my husband. As we dropped it off with some other books and got in the car to leave, a man came running out holding the manual reverently. "I've been looking for one of these books for years," he exulted. "I can't thank you enough for leaving it!"

It was one of those moments that make you feel as though you've really had a nice day.

A NEW FAD UNRAVELS
OLD MEMORIES

March 29, 2007

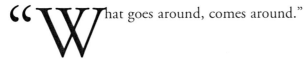

"What goes around, comes around."

The truth of that old chestnut came back to mind when I heard the recent news that knitting is hot again! Apparently knitting and crocheting are all the rage among young women. Who would have thought it would come back?

The last knitting I did was years ago when I made a small sweater and a crib blanket when my first grandchild was born. Recently, I found myself in a shop buying yarn to send as a birthday present to my youngest granddaughter, who has taken up knitting while in New York studying for her P.h.D. in art history at New York University.

It all got me to thinking about past needlework that went on when I was growing up.

Those were the days when my mother made most of my clothes. Even fancy things like a chiffon number I wore to the prom and dresses to wear to dances, when we would all go to Rhodes-On-the-Pawtuxet to hear the music of the big bands. Inevitably, I learned sewing and knitting myself, but never was as accomplished as Mother, who once ran a small yarn shop of her own.

Reading about the renaissance of needlework, I began to wonder how it all originally began. My research turned up various hypotheses. Some believe that knitting was developed prior to B.C. The basis of this idea is that the oldest examples of seemingly knitted pieces turned out to be socks with needles made of wood or bone. It is fairly much agreed that the art of hand knitting has been around for thousands of years. Various countries have been credited with its origin ... including Persia,

Israel, Jordan and Syria, while knitted socks discovered in Egyptian tombs have been dated between the 3rd and 6th centuries A.D.

Another theory is that fishermen invented knitting by using the rudiments of the practice in weaving and knotting their nets and snares. Scots claim to have the largest share of credit, while the craft was also practiced in Italy and Spain with needles made of bone, wood, or ivory. Much later, of course, needles made of steel, celluloid and plastic became staples. I can't help, however, picturing in my mind some pre-historic females sitting around a fire and trying to see which one of them could mold and polish the best looking and workable pair of bone needles. Maybe the "yarn" on hand would be coming from a slain wooly mammoth. Who knows?

For centuries, knitting and crocheting were cottage industries but, inevitably, in 1589, an inventor named William Lee came up with the first knitting machine. At that time, Mr. Lee was denied a patent by Queen Elizabeth the First, because it was feared that it would curtail the work of hand knitters. By the 19th century, power was applied to knitting machines and by the 20th century, knittedwear entered the world in every category of garments.

In addition to its value in creating useful, and quite often beautiful, articles, the activity is very relaxing. In an airport, for example, waiting for a delayed flight, some passengers have found that having a bit of knitting equipment in their carry-ons is a good way to relieve stress. As a means of passing the time, I remember having worked several times in a minor capacity in a television series and being surprised, during the long waiting periods between "takes," to find how many of the "extras" seated on the tiers of audience seats were engaged in knitting. In fact, so were quite a few of the principals, as well. Both women and even a few men.

By coincidence, during the time I was sending the present of yarn to my granddaughter, I happened to run across a box I hadn't opened since I brought my things out of storage two years ago. Inside the box I found something I'd almost forgotten about.

Wrapped in tissue paper and carefully preserved was a crocheted afghan that my late mother had been working on and nearly finished many years ago before she became ill.

Gently, I unwrapped it and spread it out on my bed. Never having been used, or submitted to light, its colors were just as vibrant as when she had first purchased the yarn. It was an emotional moment as I could almost see her once more as she had been in the last year of her life, a still-young woman at 59, sitting in her chair, deftly weaving the crochet hook and drawing the yarn in and out of the squares.

The afghan is constructed in the old-fashioned Granny pattern. All its squares are complete and woven together, but a few were somehow unraveled in their centers and need to be repaired. It probably is supposed to be finished off with a band of black woven all around the edges, too.

Since I am such a needlework klutz, I am thinking of taking the whole thing over to the nearby Senior Center and enlisting some knowledgeable person to help me out in finishing it. I'm sure my mom would be pleased, and so would I. And one day, a granddaughter will be, as well.

SHOPPING

Outside of becoming a hermit, a lighthouse keeper, or a Basque sheep herder, the life of a writer is probably the least gregarious profession one could choose. Spending days cooped up in a little room staring at four walls and four equally unresponsive rows of word processor keys can send you looking for diversion in unlikely places ... and tends to make the most pedestrian pursuit look fascinating.

The highlight of my day has often been shopping in the supermarket. Romance? Adventure? Hardly. Still, you have to take your jollies where you find them, and the writer's imagination, which may perversely falter at the desk, may work overtime elsewhere.

I wonder, for instance, about the rather shabbily dressed lady who just ordered an inch-and-a-half-thick top sirloin steak ... for eight people! What momentous event moved her to hand over a week's food money for this one meal? Visiting relatives she wishes to impress? The return of one prodigal son or daughter? The end of her diet? I envision the family sitting down to this festive repast and then eating lots of pasta and rice concoctions for the rest of the week.

The there's that man ahead of me in the checkout line with six cans of sardines, three kinds of imported cheese, a jar of horseradish, kippered herring, dill pickles ... and a loaf of bread ... probably the one thing his wife asked him to pick up on his way home.

The harassed-looking woman with the two cases of cat food and an enormous bag of kitty litter brings to mind a vivid memory of a time when we had six cats, three of them with litters of kittens ... thirteen in all. The orange tabby kept her brood in the garage; the tiger-stripe's family was ensconced in a bedroom closet, and the black one's trio in the cellar. Mealtime was a scene of bedlam ... some eating in the kitchen (the tractable ones) ... the more aggressive ones outside the back door. There were occasional snarls and now and then bits of fur flying ... How crazy can you be? But that was long ago ... and far away.

Emerging from my writing cell and yearning for human contact, I sometimes strike up conversations with strangers. Especially in the produce department, where people tend to ask my advice about fruit and vegetables. I must look like I know something, but that is a façade. Selecting a cantaloupe, for instance, I was recently consulted by several bystanders about judging its ripeness. I picked one up and sniffed it ... pronouncing it not ready yet. A gentleman disagreed, insisting that the best test was pressing the fruit, looking for a slight "give." Another customer said she put her faith in rapping on the melon and listening to the sound. Pretty soon, there we were, sniffing, pinching, and rapping like crazy. (In spite of all that, I ended up with a "lemon" of a melon.)

Since the present-day supermarket has become a virtual department store, I sometimes wander into the "literary," section that presents a variety of reading matter, mostly in the form of paperback romances and self-help books. In the latter category, publishers have used the idea of the supposed healing powers of "chicken soup" as a metaphor for an outpouring of books of short anecdotes designed to comfort all human trauma ... Guaranteed to bring a smile or a tear ... or, in some cases, a touch of tummy-upset.

Not far from the book department, I often browse through the greeting-card section, where I once came upon two slightly distraught ladies who seemed to be searching without success through the racks. "Oh, dear," one complained, "I'll never find a suitable 'Happy Birthday to my Ex-Daughter-in-Law card.' Let alone a 'Happy Housewarming to my Son and His Girlfriend.'"

"Ha!" her companion said. "You're lucky. I'm looking for a 'Happy Anniversary to my Son and his Boyfriend.'"

"Make it 'His Significant Other,'" said her friend. "That might do it."

It looks to me as though Hallmark and other card companies had better pay attention. Things change and they have to go with it. For example, to respond to a multiple birth announcement you might want to send a card reading, "Congratulations On Your Litter." Or, on the other side of the coin, there could be a demand in the get-well section for one entitled, "So You're Having a Vasectomy?" ... and for the friend who's had plastic surgery, how about, "I'll Grow Accustomed to Your Face"?

SINGING THE PC BLUES

April 28, 2005

I sit down opposite my opponent and study its face ... white and forbidding, flashing its little black signal at me. I am determined to win this time. I know you, I think to myself. You are very knowledgeable. You have unmeasured data and material available to you. Human beings can learn from you, but you can't think, and I can. I am smarter than you, and I am going to prove it.

My opponent just keeps on blinking at me. If it can laugh, it is laughing now. In its black heart it is chuckling. Go right ahead, it is thinking. After all, I'm just a tool. Everybody has told you that. You're just too dumb to know how to use me.

My opponent, of course, is my PC, my computer, and it has my number. It knows that we do not speak the same language. I speak English, it speaks Computereze, a tongue spoken fluently by every child over the age of three (maybe two), yet one that I have found very hard to master. I thought I was good at learning in school to pick at least the rudiments of Spanish, French, German, and even elementary Latin. I enjoy knowing a few words and my pronunciation received praise from my teachers. But that was many years before the electronic age that has overtaken us and left me humbled. And pretty darned mad!

The worst part is that I thought I had it all more or less under control when I first got a word processor and became adroit enough using it to write thousands of words, many of them ending up in print. It's true that there was a booklet that accompanied my WP with lots of pages that I never read. I was content just to be able to turn out columns, essays, and articles without too much stress without learning all the various options available to me. I typed, it printed, and voila! That was enough. Even after I bought a computer several years ago, and learned how to do e-mail and look up a few things on the Internet, I still did most all my writing on my trusty word processor. Then, tragedy struck. My poor old WP began to fail. First, it was the tapes, then the daisy wheel. I went through at least three daisy wheels that I thought were defective. One wouldn't print the letter "l," another balked at "u" and yet another left out the "m"s. After finishing a page of writing, I was forced to sit down and fill in the missing letters with a pen ... which ended up looking terrible, anyhow. Then the inevitable happened. The ailing machine failed utterly to perform.

I didn't give up without a fight, however. I called every possible number in the yellow pages to find somebody who might be able to fix it, or someone who might know where I could find another Brother WP Model 3550 that I might beg, borrow, or give a good home. All the people I talked to were sympathetic but in general got a good laugh out of my requests. I might as well have been looking for a horse and buggy. Actually, I might have more luck finding that. There seems to be, however, no collectors of defunct word processors ... and no old WP graveyard where they go to die.

Which brings us back to my old nemesis, the computer. I'm pretty sure it hates me and the feeling, I'm afraid, is mutual. It loses my material. It doesn't put the words where I want them to go. And the funny thing is, in the beginning, it started out rather well, I thought. When I first turned on the machine and turned on the speakers, a pleasant voice said, "Good afternoon, Virginia." I was astonished! Since then, two years have passed and the damned thing hasn't spoken to me again. I have, however, spoken to it. In words not necessarily acceptable in a family newspaper.

At risk of sounding like one of Woody Allen's old comedy routines, I have to admit to having a long-standing problem with mechanical devices. Woody would probably call it a feud with appliances. Toasters have a tendency to always burn my bread, irons get too hot and burn my clothes or never get hot enough, bathroom heaters automatically turn themselves off before the room is warm enough and won't go back on again even though the red light is still on. How mean is that?

As for automobiles, once while driving to the hospital with my pregnant daughter-in-law, whose labor pains were less than 5 minutes apart, the stick shift of her car came out of the floor into my hand. Luckily, I was able to attach it again and get her to the emergency room in time. That car never did like me, I remember.

"After the piece above came out in the paper, I received a call from a very nice lady who had the kind of word processor I was looking for. Her name is Sophie Lewis and she brought the machine out herself, installed it, and left me with discs, instructions, and extremely grateful and relieved, my sense of the kindness of strangers firmly restored.

Thank you, Sophie. There were several others who also tried to help. Muchas gracias, one and all.

And now, two years later, I am glad to say I have finally managed to become at least on speaking terms with my PC. Perhaps we may someday become fast friends and I may live to hear it greet me once again … but maybe that's asking for too much.

THE WRITING LIFE

February 24, 2000

A s one who has always been intensely interested in language and the power of words, I spend a lot of time reading and studying the style of various writers in the field of non-fiction, especially good essayists and columnists. I enjoy the economy of their work; their ability to convey ideas, evoke emotions, and promote thoughtful contemplation within the confines of the limited word space in a magazine or newspaper.

Russell Baker, whose "Observer" column appeared on the op-ed pages of *The New York Times* for so many years and who won a Pulitzer Prize for commentary, is one of those. His longtime best-selling memoir, "Growing Up," has been on my bookshelf since it first appeared twenty years ago. I often go back to re-reading it and always find new things to admire.

The same may be said about the works of the late E.B. White, famed for his essays in the early New Yorker magazine and many books, including his revised edition of William Strunk Jr.'s "Elements of Style," the essential manual for all serious practitioners of good writing.

It appears to me that the difference between an essay and a column is mostly length and depth. A column is a form of brief essay, a condensed version, if you will. A bite instead of a whole cookie. In many cases, the point or focus used in any column could be expanded into essay format; the subject explored and embellished. The column has the requirements of catching the reader's interest, illustrating its theme and tying up the package with a satisfactory closing.

In an essay, the writer has a lot more time and leeway to be fanciful or down-to-earth, philosophical or scientific ... whatever the subject matter allows or demands. Often, the writer's skill is more important than the subject. A good writer can hold the reader enthralled with words and mental pictures about things he or she normally could care less about. In my case, such as sports. Although I have no interest in athletics, occasionally I enjoy reading colorful articles in the Sports section because of the writer's use of language.

Writing is one thing but getting published, as they say, is a horse of a different color. Many are the writers who eventually achieved fame and fortune whose works were first met with rejection, including James Joyce, Edgar Allen Poe, Zane Grey, and Walt Whitman. James Joyce's "Dubliners" was rejected 22 times before a publisher took a chance on it. These renowned authors also share another bond; they were all originally self publishers.

Poe, at one time, came out his own copy of "Tamerland and Other Poems." Only forty copies were sold, and he made less than a dollar after expenses. A century later, one of those copies sold for $11,000. Henry David Thoreau, whose self-published thousand copies of his book, "A Week on the Concord and Merrimack Rivers," sold so poorly that Thoreau ended up writing in his journal, "I now have a library of nearly nine hundred volumes, over seven hundred of which I wrote myself."

Of course there are also many success stories of writers who self-published. One of these was Richard Paul Evans whose slim volume, "The Christmas Box," has sold millions of copies and was made into a movie for television. Another blockbuster of self-publishing was first-time author James Redfield's spiritual parable, "The Celestine Prophecy," which remained on *The New York Times* best-seller list for over three years.

The above are admittedly few and far between, and it's probably that for every winner in the business of self-publishing, there are thousands of writers who end up with a garage full of unsold volumes. To others, the whole thing may be an adventure, the achievement of having a book of theirs in print to justify the means ... with few regrets.

After vowing for years to never think about publishing my own stuff, I am now giving that enterprise serious consideration. Not with a so-called vanity press, which requires a fee for services, but with a print on demand, or POD outfit, which allows the writer to order and pay for as many or few volumes as desired and leaves all selling and rights in his/her hands.

While I've had considerable modest luck over the years finding markets for my work with articles, columns, essays, and such, as yet publishers have failed to woo me with contracts for books. So now I am thinking about publishing myself, starting with a collection of these columns called Rhyme and Reason, under the title, The Cranky Yankee. I just hope I don't find myself in the same sorry situation as poor Henry David Thoreau with all the un-sold volumes.

Come to think of it, though, he didn't do so badly in the end, did he?

I should be so lucky!

Some time ago, while a resident of California, I became so homesick for New England that I wrote a sentimental essay that has
remained hidden away, unprinted for decades.

Time may have made some of it obsolete, but here it is. My
Thanksgiving piece out of the closet at last.

MY NEW ENGLAND

November 24, 2004

I am a New Englander. New England that is born and bred in the bone. Passed down from generations long gone. From ancestors who captained ships and sailed after whales all the way to New Zealand and 'round the Horn. I went out there to California for a new way of life ... to see the world ... and I found that it is a good place, but not for a New Englander. There is another song I hear always, and this is how it goes:

Oh, Boston is a codfish town, a baked bean town, a brown bread town. A cosmopolitan city with narrow winding streets. With big department stores and little exclusive shops where the old families trade. There's Fanueil Hall, the Freedom Trail and the waterfront ... The Public Garden, Louisburg Square, the old brownstones and the Esplanade, where you walk along the river in the evening and maybe take a little boat ride. And here, in July, tired men lie on the grass with newspapers over their faces and lovers lie close together, not caring about the heat, and apartment dwellers walk their dogs endlessly ... and in the evening they all come to hear the concerts in the Shell and slap at the mosquitoes.

There is good food in Boston. The Parker House, the lobster houses and oyster houses ... and the places where you walk in through the kitchen and sit down, family style, and eat all you can hold. Plenty of cocktail lounges, too, where you can sit and tell lies and hear them told over Manhattans. If you want, you can go see the old landmarks – Bunker Hill and the Old North Church where Paul Revere's lantern hung. Then you can feel the ghosts. Stiff-necked Puritans and rugged Patriots who dumped the tea overboard and homesick British soldiers in red coats who wanted to get it over with and go home. Then there are the colleges – MIT and Tufts and dear old Harvard and generations of young men who sing old songs and dream old dreams.

Rhode Island is where I come from, mostly. Providence is a jonny-cake town, a clambake town, a chowder town. It has a downtown with lots of old buildings and little streets almost European. Soon, there is bound to be a makeover of the city's heartland, but I hope they will spare the antique qualities. There is the majestic State House, the lovely Roger Williams Park, Narragansett Bay and the East Side, where the fine old houses stand, carefully restored. There is Brown University and Rhode Island College and the Rhode Island School of Design. Further out, there is South County, green and lovely, with the rocky New England farmlands stretching down to meet the sea, and Narragansett Pier and Newport, the playground of the rich, haunted by the ghosts of hardheaded old tycoons and their mansions.

New Bedford, Massachusetts is a good place for ghosts – ghosts of the old whaling ships coming in from their voyages after years away from home, loaded with their rich, smelly cargo and their tired, weather-beaten crew. There were always some who didn't come home, of course. Whales were very costly.

Up in Gloucester you can find them, too. You can walk along the waterfront where the fishing fleets put out for the Grand Banks off Newfoundland, down among the shacks where the Portuguese fisherman live and along the docks. You can look out and feel the weight of those who lived by the sea and died by it.

Down on Cape Cod there are ghosts. But you won't find them rolling down the roads in the warm, mellow days of summer, through the cranberry bogs and past the canal, the picturesque towns and the sandy dunes. To find them you must wait until the tourist season is over and all the quaint little restaurants, gift shops and summer theaters are closed and visitors have gone back to the city.

You must look for them in the bleak days of November when the skies are gray and overcast and the wind that sweeps in from the salty marshes is biting, with the first snowflakes in it. Then you can stand on some lonely beach and feel what it must have been like to be a Pilgrim, to be a stranger and land upon that unfriendly shore and see nothing but wilderness, immense, overwhelming, for ever and ever.

You can go through the pretty little towns of Connecticut with their white, graceful, spired churches and the names that roll easily on the tongue: Mystic, Guilford, Old Lyme and on up through the mill towns of Massachusetts: Lowell, Lawrence, the lovely Berkshiresand through the green hills of Vermont with the sugar maples, the lakes, the rugged, pine-scented mountains of New Hampshire and the vast silent forests and craggy shores of the state of Maine.

New England is the white glistening blanket of winter, sharp and crunchy underfoot. The smell of Christmas trees and mince pies and turkeys roasting, the sizzle of steam in radiators and the pain of frost-bitten toes and the unforgettable thrill of a sled on a downward slide. It is the rush of the melting snow down the mountain streams in March and the wild, sweet smell of the woods in spring, when the violets, trilliums and ladies slippers bloom. It is the trout, caught and cooked beside the mossy brook bank. It is the winds of March, the soft rain of April and the wild, rare arbutus of May. It is the Fourth of July, the heavy heat of August and the violent, cooling thunderstorm. It is the golden haze of Indian summer, with the shocks of hay standing neatly bundled in the fields. It is the sadness and glory of the October hills, when the dying year puts forth its most breathtaking beauty. It is the pumpkin and the wild grape and the Indian corn and the first Thanksgiving.

It is the dream, the hope, the struggle, the beginning of freedom, the heart of America.

Printed in the United States
202268BV00003B/1-90/P